MANHATTAN PREP

Number Properties

GMAT Strategy Guide

This foundational guide provides a comprehensive analysis of the properties and rules of integers tested on the GMAT. Learn, practice, and master everything from prime products to perfect squares.

guide **5**

Number Properties GMAT Strategy Guide, Sixth Edition

10-digit International Standard Book Number: 1-941234-05-4
13-digit International Standard Book Number: 978-1-941234-05-1
eISBN: 978-1-941234-26-6

Layout Design: Dan McNaney and Cathy Huang
Cover Design: Dan McNaney and Frank Callaghan
Cover Photography: Alli Ugosoli

SUSTAINABLE FORESTRY INITIATIVE   Certified Sourcing   www.sfiprogram.org   SFI-00756

INSTRUCTIONAL GUIDE SERIES

SUPPLEMENTAL GUIDE SERIES

December 2nd, 2014

Dear Student,

Thank you for picking up a copy of *Number Properties*. I hope this book gives you just the guidance you need to get the most out of your GMAT studies.

A great number of people were involved in the creation of the book you are holding. First and foremost is Zeke Vanderhoek, the founder of Manhattan Prep. Zeke was a lone tutor in New York City when he started the company in 2000. Now, well over a decade later, the company contributes to the successes of thousands of students around the globe every year.

Our Manhattan Prep Strategy Guides are based on the continuing experiences of our instructors and students. The overall vision of the 6th Edition GMAT guides was developed by Stacey Koprince, Whitney Garner, and Dave Mahler over the course of many months; Stacey and Dave then led the execution of that vision as the primary author and editor, respectively, of this book. Numerous other instructors made contributions large and small, but I'd like to send particular thanks to Josh Braslow, Kim Cabot, Dmitry Farber, Ron Purewal, Emily Meredith Sledge, and Ryan Starr. Dan McNaney and Cathy Huang provided design and layout expertise as Dan managed book production, while Liz Krisher made sure that all the moving pieces, both inside and outside of our company, came together at just the right time. Finally, we are indebted to all of the Manhattan Prep students who have given us feedback over the years. This book wouldn't be half of what it is without your voice.

At Manhattan Prep, we aspire to provide the best instructors and resources possible, and we hope that you will find our commitment manifest in this book. We strive to keep our books free of errors, but if you think we've goofed, please post to manhattanprep.com/GMAT/errata. If you have any questions or comments in general, please email our Student Services team at gmat@manhattanprep.com. Or give us a shout at 212-721-7400 (or 800-576-4628 in the U.S. or Canada). I look forward to hearing from you.

Thanks again, and best of luck preparing for the GMAT!

Sincerely,

Chris Ryan
Vice President of Academics
Manhattan Prep

HOW TO ACCESS YOUR ONLINE RESOURCES

IF YOU ARE A REGISTERED MANHATTAN PREP STUDENT

and have received this book as part of your course materials, you have AUTOMATIC access to ALL of our online resources. This includes all practice exams, question banks, and online updates to this book. To access these resources, follow the instructions in the Welcome Guide provided to you at the start of your program. Do NOT follow the instructions below.

IF YOU PURCHASED THIS BOOK FROM MANHATTANPREP.COM OR AT ONE OF OUR CENTERS

1. Go to: **www.manhattanprep.com/gmat/studentcenter**
2. Log in with the username and password you chose when setting up your account.

IF YOU PURCHASED THIS BOOK AT A RETAIL LOCATION

1. Go to: **www.manhattanprep.com/gmat/access**
2. Create an account or, if you already have one, log in on this page with your username and password.
3. Follow the instructions on the screen.

Your one year of online access begins on the day that you register your book at the above URL.

You only need to register your product ONCE at the above URL. To use your online resources any time AFTER you have completed the registration process, log in to the following URL:

www.manhattanprep.com/gmat/studentcenter

Please note that online access is nontransferable. This means that only NEW and UNREGISTERED copies of the book will grant you online access. Previously used books will NOT provide any online resources.

IF YOU PURCHASED AN EBOOK VERSION OF THIS BOOK

1. Create an account with Manhattan Prep at this website:

www.manhattanprep.com/gmat/register

2. Email a copy of your purchase receipt to **gmat@manhattanprep.com** to activate your resources. Please be sure to use the same email address to create an account that you used to purchase the eBook.

For any questions, email **gmat@manhattanprep.com** or call **800-576-4628**.

Please refer to the following page for a description of the online resources that come with this book.

YOUR ONLINE RESOURCES
YOUR PURCHASE INCLUDES ONLINE ACCESS TO THE FOLLOWING:

6 FULL-LENGTH GMAT PRACTICE EXAMS

The 6 full-length GMAT practice exams included with the purchase of this book are delivered online using Manhattan Prep's proprietary computer-adaptive test engine. The exams adapt to your ability level by drawing from a bank of more than 1,200 unique questions of varying difficulty levels written by Manhattan Prep's expert instructors, all of whom have scored in the 99th percentile on the Official GMAT. At the end of each exam you will receive a score, an analysis of your results, and the opportunity to review detailed explanations for each question. You may choose to take the exams timed or untimed.

Important Note: The 6 GMAT exams included with the purchase of this book are the SAME exams that you receive upon purchasing ANY book in the Manhattan Prep GMAT Complete Strategy Guide Set.

5 FREE INTERACT™ LESSONS

Interact™ is a comprehensive self-study program that is fun, intuitive, and directed by you. Each interactive video lesson is taught by an expert Manhattan Prep instructor and includes dozens of individual branching points. The choices you make define the content you see. This book comes with access to the first five lessons of GMAT Interact. Lessons are available on your computer or iPad so you can prep where you are, when you want. For more information on the full version of this program, visit **manhattanprep.com/gmat/interact**

NUMBER PROPERTIES ONLINE QUESTION BANK

The Online Question Bank for Number Properties consists of 25 extra practice questions (with detailed explanations) that test the variety of concepts and skills covered in this book. These questions provide you with extra practice beyond the problem sets contained in this book. You may use our online timer to practice your pacing by setting time limits for each question in the bank.

ONLINE UPDATES TO THE CONTENT IN THIS BOOK

The content presented in this book is updated periodically to ensure that it reflects the GMAT's most current trends. You may view all updates, including any known errors or changes, upon registering for online access.

The above resources can be found in your Student Center at manhattanprep.com/gmat/studentcenter

TABLE *of* CONTENTS

Official Guide Problem Sets

As you work through this strategy guide, it is a very good idea to test your skills using official problems that appeared on the real GMAT in the past. To help you with this step of your studies, we have classified all of the problems from the three main *Official Guide* books and devised some problem sets to accompany this book.

These problem sets live in your Manhattan Prep Student Center so that they can be updated whenever the test makers update their books. When you log into your Student Center, click on the link for the *Official Guide Problem Sets*, found on your home page. Download them today!

The problem sets consist of three broad groups of questions:

1. A final quiz: Take this quiz after completing this entire guide.

2. A full practice set of questions: If you are taking one of our classes, this is the homework given on your syllabus, so just follow the syllabus assignments. If you are not taking one of our classes, you can do this practice set whenever you feel that you have a very solid understanding of the material taught in this guide.

3. A full reference list of all *Official Guide* problems that test the topics covered in this strategy guide: Use these problems to test yourself on specific topics or to create larger sets of mixed questions.

As you begin studying, try one problem at a time and review it thoroughly before moving on. In the middle of your studies, attempt some mixed sets of problems from a small pool of topics (the two quizzes we've devised for you are good examples of how to do this). Later in your studies, mix topics from multiple guides and include some questions that you've chosen randomly out of the *Official Guide*. This way, you'll learn to be prepared for anything!

Study Tips:

1. DO time yourself when answering questions.

2. DO cut yourself off and make a guess if a question is taking too long. You can try it again later without a time limit, but first practice the behavior you want to exhibit on the real test: let go and move on.

3. DON'T answer all of the *Official Guide* questions by topic or chapter at once. The real test will toss topics at you in random order, and half of the battle is figuring out what each new question is testing. Set yourself up to learn this when doing practice sets.

Chapter 1
of
Number Properties

Divisibility & Primes

Here are some more examples:

$8 \div 2 = 4$	Therefore, 8 is divisible by 2.
	You can also say that 2 is a **divisor** or **factor** of 8.
$2 \div 8 = 0.25$	Therefore, 2 is *not* divisible by 8.
$(-6) \div 2 = -3$	Therefore, -6 is divisible by 2.
$(-6) \div (-4) = 1.5$	Therefore, -6 is *not* divisible by -4.

Rules of Divisibility by Certain Integers

The **divisibility rules** are very useful shortcuts to determine whether an integer is divisible by 2, 3, 4, 5, 6, 8, 9, and 10.

An integer is divisible by:

2 if the integer is even.
12 is divisible by 2, but 13 is not. Integers that are divisible by 2 are called *even* and integers that are not are called *odd*. You can tell whether a number is even by checking to see whether the units (ones) digit is 0, 2, 4, 6, or 8. For example, 1,234,567 is odd, because 7 is odd, whereas 2,345,678 is even, because 8 is even.

3 if the sum of the integer's digits is divisible by 3.
72 is divisible by 3 because the sum of its digits is $7 + 2 = 9$, which is divisible by 3. By contrast, 83 is not divisible by 3, because the sum of its digits is 11, which is not divisible by 3.

4 if the integer is divisible by 2 *twice*, or if the last two digits are divisible by 4.
28 is divisible by 4 because you can divide it by 2 twice and get an integer result ($28 \div 2 = 14$, and $14 \div 2 = 7$). For larger numbers, check only the last two digits. For example, 23,456 is divisible by 4 because 56 is divisible by 4, but 25,678 is not divisible by 4 because 78 is not divisible by 4.

5 if the integer ends in 0 or 5.
75 and 80 are divisible by 5, but 77 and 83 are not.

6 if the integer is divisible by *both* 2 and 3.
48 is divisible by 6 since it is divisible by 2 (it ends with an 8, which is even) AND by 3 ($4 + 8 = 12$, which is divisible by 3).

8 if the integer is divisible by 2 three times, or if the last three digits are divisible by 8.
32 is divisible by 8 since you can divide it by 2 three times and get an integer result ($32 \div 2 = 16$, $16 \div 2 = 8$, and $8 \div 2 = 4$). For larger numbers, check only the last three digits. For example, 23,456 is divisible by 8 because 456 is divisible by 8, whereas 23,556 is not divisible by 8 because 556 is not divisible by 8.

9 if the sum of the integer's digits is divisible by 9.

4,185 is divisible by 9 since the sum of its digits is $4 + 1 + 8 + 5 = 18$, which is divisible by 9. By contrast, 3,459 is not divisible by 9, because the sum of its digits is 21, which is not divisible by 9.

10 if the integer ends in 0.

670 is divisible by 10, but 675 is not.

The GMAT can also test these divisibility rules in reverse. For example, if you are told that a number has a ones digit equal to 0, you can infer that that number is divisible by 10. Similarly, if you are told that the sum of the digits of x is equal to 21, you can infer that x is divisible by 3 but *not* by 9.

Note also that there is no rule listed for divisibility by 7. The simplest way to check for divisibility by 7, or by any other number not found in this list, is to perform long division.

Factors and Multiples

Factors and multiples are essentially opposite terms.

A **factor** is a positive integer that divides evenly into an integer. For example, 1, 2, 4, and 8 are all the factors (also called divisors) of 8. A factor of an integer is smaller than or equal to that integer.

A **multiple** of an integer is formed by multiplying that integer by any integer, so 8, 16, 24, and 32 are some of the multiples of 8. On the GMAT, multiples of an integer are equal to or larger than that integer.

Note that an integer is always both a factor and a multiple of itself, and that 1 is a factor of *every* integer.

An easy way to find all the factors of a *small* integers is to use **factor pairs**. Factor pairs for any integer are the pairs of factors that, when multiplied together, yield that integer. For instance, the factor pairs of 8 are (1, 8) and (2, 4).

To find the factor pairs of a number such as 72, start with the automatic factors: 1 and 72 (the number itself). Then, "walk upwards" from 1, testing to see whether different numbers are factors of 72. Once you find a number that is a factor of 72, find its partner by dividing 72 by the factor. Keep walking upwards until all factors are exhausted.

Step by step:

Small	Large
1	72
2	36
3	24
4	18
6	12
8	9

1. Make a table with two columns labeled *Small* and *Large*.

2. Start with 1 in the Small column and 72 in the Large column.

3. Test the next possible factor of 72 (which is 2); 2 is a factor of 72, so write 2 underneath the 1 in your table. Divide 72 by 2 to find the factor pair: 36. Write 36 in the Large column.

4. Repeat this process until the numbers in the Small and the Large columns run into each other. In this case, once you have tested 8 and found that 9 is its paired factor, you can stop.

Fewer Factors, More Multiples

It can be easy to confuse factors and multiples. The mnemonic "Fewer Factors, More Multiples" can help you remember the difference. Every positive integer has a limited number of factors. Factors divide into the integer and are therefore less than or equal to the integer. For example, there are only four factors of 8: 1, 2, 4, and 8.

By contrast, every positive integer has infinite multiples. These multiply out from the integer and are therefore greater than or equal to to the integer. For example, the first five multiples of 8 are 8, 16, 24, 32, and 40, but you could go on listing multiples of 8 forever.

Factors, multiples, and divisibility are very closely related concepts. For example, 3 is a factor of 12. This is the same as saying that 12 is a multiple of 3, or that 12 is divisible by 3.

On the GMAT, this terminology is often used interchangeably in order to make the problem seem harder than it actually is. Be aware of the different ways that the GMAT can phrase information about divisibility. Moreover, try to convert all such statements to the same terminology. For example, all of the following statements *say exactly the same thing*:

- 12 is divisible by 3.
- 12 is a multiple of 3.
- $\frac{12}{3}$ is an integer.
- 12 is equal to 3n, where n is an integer.
- 12 items can be shared among 3 people so that each person has the same number of items.

- 3 is a divisor of 12, or 3 is a factor of 12.
- 3 divides 12.
- $\frac{12}{3}$ yields a remainder of 0.
- 3 "goes into" 12 evenly.

Divisibility and Addition/Subtraction

If you add two multiples of 7, you get another multiple of 7. Try it: 35 + 21 = 56. This is always mathematically valid $(5 \times 7) + (3 \times 7) = (5 + 3) \times 7 = 8 \times 7$.

Likewise, if you subtract two multiples of 7, you get another multiple of 7. Try it: 35 − 21 = 14. Again, you can see why: $(5 \times 7) − (3 \times 7) = (5 − 3) \times 7 = 2 \times 7$.

This pattern holds true for the multiples of any integer N. If you add or subtract multiples of N, the result is a multiple of N. You can restate this principle using any of the disguises above: for instance, if N is a divisor of x and of y, then N is a divisor of $x + y$.

MANHATTAN
PREP

Primes

Prime numbers are a very important topic on the GMAT. A prime number is any positive integer with exactly two different factors: 1 and itself. In other words, a prime number has *no* factors other than 1 and itself. For example, 7 is prime because the only factors of 7 are 1 and 7. However, 8 is not prime because it is divisible by 2 and 4.

Note that the number 1 is not prime, as it has only one factor (itself). The first prime number is 2, which is also the only even prime. The first ten prime numbers are 2, 3, 5, 7, 11, 13, 17, 19, 23, and 29. Memorizing these primes will save you time on the test.

Prime Factorization

Breaking a number down to its prime factors can be very useful on the GMAT. Create a prime factor tree, as shown below with the number 72. Test different numbers to see which ones "go into" 72 without leaving a remainder. Once you find such a number, then split 72 into factors. For example, 72 is divisible by 6, so it can be split into 6 and 72 ÷ 6, or 12. Then repeat this process on 6 and 12 until every branch on the tree ends at a prime number. Once you have only primes, stop, because you cannot split prime numbers into two smaller factors. In this example, 72 splits into 5 total prime factors (including repeats): $2 \times 3 \times 2 \times 2 \times 3$.

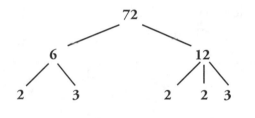

Prime factorization is an extremely important tool to use on the GMAT. Once you know the prime factors of a number, you can determine *all* the factors of that number, even large numbers. The factors can be found by building all the possible products of the prime factors.

Factor Foundation Rule

The GMAT expects you to know the **factor foundation rule: if *a* is a factor of *b*, and *b* is a factor of *c*, then *a* is a factor of *c*.** In other words, any integer is divisible by all of its factors—and it is also divisible by all of the *factors* of its factors.

For example, if 72 is divisible by 12, then 72 is also divisible by all the factors of 12 (1, 2, 3, 4, 6, and 12). Written another way, if 12 is a factor of 72, then all the factors of 12 are also factors of 72. The factor foundation rule allows you to conceive of factors as building blocks in a foundation; for example, 12 and 6 are factors, or building blocks, of 72 (because 12×6 builds 72).

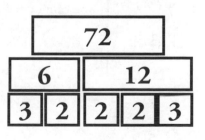

1

The number 12, in turn, is built from its own factors; for example, 4×3 builds 12. Thus, if 12 is part of the foundation of 72 and 12 in turn rests on the foundation built by its prime factors (2, 2, and 3), then 72 is also built on the foundation of 2, 2, and 3.

Going further, you can build almost any factor of 72 out of the bottom level of the foundation. For instance, 8 is a factor of 72, because you can build 8 out of the three 2's in the bottom row ($8 = 2 \times 2 \times 2$).

It is *almost* any factor, however, because one of the factors cannot be built out of the building blocks in the foundation: the number 1. Remember that the number 1 is not prime, but it is still a factor of every integer. Except for the number 1, every factor of 72 can be built out of the lowest level of 72 building blocks.

The Prime Box

The easiest way to work with the factor foundation rule is with a tool called a prime box. A **prime box** is exactly what its name implies: a box that holds all the prime factors of a number (in other words, the lowest-level building blocks). Here are prime boxes for 72, 12, and 125:

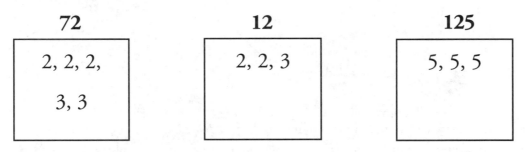

72	12	125
2, 2, 2, 3, 3	2, 2, 3	5, 5, 5

Notice that you must repeat copies of the prime factors if the number has multiple copies of that prime factor. You can use the prime box to test whether or not a specific number is a factor of another number. For example:

Is 27 a factor of 72?

72

2, 2, 2,

3, 3

For instance, $27 = 3 \times 3 \times 3$, but 72 only has *two* 3's in its prime box. Therefore, you cannot make 27 from the prime factors of 72; 27 is not a factor of 72.

Given that the integer n is divisible by 8 and 15, is n divisible by 12?

n

$$2, 2, 2,$$
$$3, 5,$$
$$\dots ?$$

First, factor both numbers: $8 = 2 \times 2 \times 2$ and $15 = 3 \times 5$. Although you don't know what n is, n has to be divisible by any number made up of those primes.

Because $12 = 2 \times 2 \times 3$, then yes, n is also divisible by 12.

Notice the ellipses and question mark ("... ?") in the prime box of n. This indicates that you have created a **partial prime box** of n. Whereas the *complete* set of prime factors of 72 can be calculated and put into its prime box, you only have a *partial* list of prime factors of n, because n is an unknown number. You know that n is divisible by 8 and 15, but you do *not* know what additional primes, if any, n has in its prime box.

Most of the time, when building a prime box for a *variable*, you will use a partial prime box, but when building a prime box for a *number*, you will use a complete prime box.

Remainders

Most of this chapter has focused on numbers that are divisible by other numbers (factors). This section, however, discusses what happens when a number, such as 8, is divided by a *non*-factor, such as 5.

Every division has four parts:

1. The **dividend** is the number being divided. In $8 \div 5$, the dividend is 8.

2. The **divisor** is the number that is dividing. In $8 \div 5$, the divisor is 5.

3. The **quotient** is the number of times that the divisor goes into the dividend *completely*. The quotient is always an integer. In $8 \div 5$, the quotient is 1 because 5 goes into 8 one (1) time completely.

4. The **remainder** is what is left over if the dividend is not divisible by the divisor. In $8 \div 5$, the remainder is 3 because 3 is left over after 5 goes into 8 once.

Putting it all together, you have $8 \div 5 = 1$, with a remainder of 3.

As another example, the number 17 is not divisible by 5. When you divide 17 by 5 using long division, you get 3 with a remainder of 2:

$$\begin{array}{r} 3 \\ 5\overline{)17} \\ -15 \\ \hline 2 \end{array}$$

The quotient is 3 because 15 is the largest multiple of 5 smaller than 17, and 15 ÷ 5 = 3. The remainder is 2 because 17 is 2 more than a multiple of 5 (15).

You can also express this relationship as a general formula:

Dividend = Quotient × Divisor + Remainder
(or, Dividend = Multiple of Divisor + Remainder)

Problem Set

For questions #1–6, answer each question Yes, No, or Cannot Be Determined. If your answer is Cannot Be Determined, use two numerical examples to show how the problem could go either way. All variables in problems #1–6 are assumed to be integers.

1. If a is divided by 7 or by 18, an integer results. Is $\dfrac{a}{42}$ an integer?

2. If 80 is a factor of r, is 15 a factor of r?

3. Given that 7 is a factor of n and 7 is a factor of p, is $n + p$ divisible by 7?

4. If j is divisible by 12 and 10, is j divisible by 24?

5. Given that 6 is a divisor of r and r is a factor of s, is 6 a factor of s?

6. If s is a multiple of 12 and t is a multiple of 12, is $7s + 5t$ a multiple of 12?

Save the below problem set for review, either after you finish this book or after you finish all of the Quant books that you plan to study.

7. A skeet shooting competition awards prizes for each round as follows: the first-place winner receives 11 points, the second-place winner receives 7 points, the third-place finisher receives 5 points, and the fourth-place finisher receives 2 points. No other prizes are awarded. Johan competes in several rounds of the skeet shooting competition and receives points every time he competes. If the product of all of the points he receives equals 84,700, in how many rounds does he participate?

8. If x, y, and z are integers, is x even?

    (1) $10^x = (4^y)(5^z)$
    (2) $3^{x+5} = 27^{y+1}$

Solutions

1. Yes:

a

2, 3, 3, 7, … ?

If *a* is divisible by 7 and by 18, its prime factors include 2, 3, 3, and 7, as indicated by the prime box to the left. Therefore, any integer that can be constructed as a product of any of these prime factors is also a factor of *a*. Factoring 42, you get = 2 × 3 × 7. Therefore, 42 is also a factor of *a*.

2. Cannot Be Determined:

r

2, 2, 2, 2, 5,…?

If *r* is divisible by 80, its prime factors include 2, 2, 2, 2, and 5, as indicated by the prime box to the left. Therefore, any integer that can be constructed as a product of any of these prime factors is also a factor of *r*. Factoring 15, you get 3 × 5. Since you don't know whether the prime factor 3 is in the prime box, you cannot determine whether 15 is a factor of *r*. As numerical examples, you could take *r* = 80, in which case 15 is *not* a factor of *r*, or *r* = 240, in which case 15 *is* a factor of *r*.

3. Yes: If two numbers are both multiples of the same number, then their *sum* is also a multiple of that same number. Since *n* and *p* share the common factor 7, the sum of *n* and *p* must also be divisible by 7.

4. Cannot Be Determined:

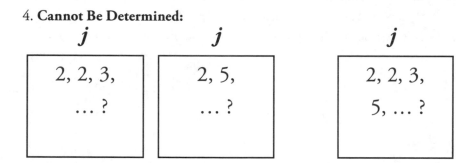

If *j* is divisible by 12 and by 10, its prime factors include 2, 2, 3, and 5, as indicated by the prime box to the left. What is the minimum number of 2's necessary to create 12 or 10? You need two 2's to create 12. You could use one of those same 2's to create the 10. Therefore, there are only *two* 2's that are definitely in the prime factorization of *j*, because the 2 in the prime factorization of 10 may be *redundant*—that is, it may be the *same* 2 as one of the 2's in the prime factorization of 12.

Factoring 24, you get 2 × 2 × 2 × 3. The prime box of *j* contains at least two 2's and could contain more. The number 24 requires three 2's. Therefore, you may or may not be able to create 24 from *j*'s prime box; 24 is not necessarily a factor of *j*.

1

As another way to prove that you cannot determine whether 24 is a factor of j, consider 60. The number 60 is divisible by both 12 and 10. However, it is *not* divisible by 24. Therefore, j could equal 60, in which case it is not divisible by 24. Alternatively, j could equal 120, in which case it *is* divisible by 24.

5. **Yes:** By the factor foundation rule, if 6 is a factor of r and r is a factor of s, then 6 is a factor of s.

6. **Yes:** If s is a multiple of 12, then so is $7s$. If t is a multiple of 12, then so is $5t$. Since $7s$ and $5t$ are both multiples of 12, then their sum $(7s + 5t)$ is also a multiple of 12.

7. **7 rounds:** Notice that the values for scoring first, second, third, and fourth place in the competition are all prime numbers. Notice also that the *product* of all of the scores Johan received is known. Therefore, if you simply take the prime factorization of the product of his scores, you can determine what scores he received (and how many scores he received):

$$84{,}700 = 847 \times 100 = 7 \times 121 \times 2 \times 2 \times 5 \times 5 = 7 \times 11 \times 11 \times 2 \times 2 \times 5 \times 5$$

Thus, Johan received first place twice (11 points each), second place once (7 points each), third place twice (5 points each), and fourth place twice (2 points each.) He received a prize 7 times, so he competed in 7 rounds.

8. **(A):** (1) SUFFICIENT: Statement (1) tells you that $10^x = (4^y)(5^z)$. You can break the bases down into prime factors: $(2 \times 5)^x = (2^2)^y \times 5^z = 2^{2y} \times 5^z$. This tells you that $x = 2y$ and $x = z$. (You need the same number of 2's and the same number of 5's on either side of the equation.) Since you know y is an integer, x must be even, because $x = 2y$.

(2) INSUFFICIENT: Statement (2) tells you that $3^{x+5} = 27^{y+1}$. You can again break the bases down into prime factors: $3^{x+5} = (3^3)^{y+1}$, so $3^{x+5} = 3^{3(y+1)}$. This tells you that $x + 5 = 3y + 3$, so $x = 3y - 2$. (Again, you need the same number of 3's on either side of the equation.) Since y is an integer, x must be 2 smaller than a multiple of 3, but that does not tell you whether x is even. If $y = 1$, then $x = 1$ (odd), but if $y = 2$, then $x = 4$ (even).

Chapter 2 of
Number Properties

Odds, Evens, Positives, & Negatives

In This Chapter...

Chapter 2

Odds, Evens, Positives, & Negatives

Even numbers are integers that are divisible by 2. Odd numbers are integers that are not divisible by 2. All integers are either even or odd. For example:

Evens: 0, 2, 4, 6, 8, 10, 12 …   Odds: 1, 3, 5, 7, 9, 11 …

Consecutive integers alternate between even and odd: 9, 10, 11, 12, 13 …
                                                            O, E, O, E, O …

Negative integers are also either even or odd:

Evens: −2, −4, −6, −8, −10, −12 …   Odds: −1, −3, −5, −7, −9, −11 …

Arithmetic Rules of Odds & Evens

The GMAT tests your knowledge of how odd and even numbers combine through addition, subtraction, multiplication, and division. Rules for adding, subtracting, multiplying, and dividing odd and even numbers can be derived by testing out simple numbers, but it pays to memorize the following rules for operating with odds and evens, as they are extremely useful for certain GMAT math questions.

Addition and subtraction:

Even ± Even = Even $8 + 6 = 14$
Odd ± Odd = Even $7 + 9 = 16$
Even ± Odd = Odd $7 + 8 = 15$

If they're the same, the sum (or difference) will be even. If they're different, the sum (or difference) will be odd.

Multiplication:

Even × Even = Even	$2 \times 4 = 8$
Even × Odd = Even	$4 \times 3 = 12$
Odd × Odd = Odd	$3 \times 5 = 15$

If one even number is present, the product will be even. If you have only odd numbers, the product will be odd.

If you multiply together several even integers, the result will be divisible by higher and higher powers of 2 because each even number will contribute at least one 2 to the factors of the product.

For example, if there are two even integers in a set of integers being multipled together, the result will be divisible by 4:

$$\mathbf{2} \times 5 \times \mathbf{6} = 60 \qquad \text{(divisible by 4)}$$

If there are three even integers in a set of integers being multipled together, the result will be divisible by 8:

$$\mathbf{2} \times 5 \times \mathbf{6} \times \mathbf{10} = 600 \qquad \text{(divisible by 8)}$$

Division:

There are no guaranteed outcomes in division, because the division of two integers may not yield an integer result. In these cases, you'll have to try the actual numbers given. The divisibility tools outlined in Chapter 1 can help you determine the outcome.

Representing Odds & Evens Algebraically

Try this problem:

Is positive integer m odd?

(1) $m = 2k + 1$, where k is an integer.
(2) m is a multiple of 3.

Statement (2) is easier to attack. The variable m could be 3, which is odd, or 6, which is even. This statement is NOT sufficient.

Statement (1) is a bit trickier. An even number is a multiple of 2, so any even number can be represented as $2n$, where n is an integer. An odd number is always one more than an even number, so the subsequent odd number could be written $2n + 1$. This notation is a signal that you have an odd integer!

If $m = 2k + 1$, where k is an integer, then m must be odd. Statement (1) is sufficient to answer the question.

The answer is (**A**).

The GMAT will sometimes use this notation to disguise information about odds and evens; keep an eye out for it!

2

Positives & Negatives

Numbers can be either positive or negative (except the number 0, which is neither):

$$-5 \quad -4 \quad -3 \quad -2 \quad -1 \quad 0 \quad 1 \quad 2 \quad 3 \quad 4 \quad 5$$

Negative numbers are all to the left of the number 0. Positive numbers are all to the right of the number 0.

Note that a variable (such as x) can have either a positive or a negative value, unless there is evidence otherwise. The variable x is not necessarily positive, nor is $-x$ necessarily negative. For example, if $x = -3$, then $-x = 3$.

Absolute Value: Absolutely Positive

The absolute value of a number answers this question: How far away is the number from 0 on the number line? For example, the number 5 is exactly 5 units away from 0, so the absolute value of 5 equals 5. Mathematically, this is written using the symbol for absolute value: $|5| = 5$. To find the absolute value of -5, look at the number line above: -5 is also exactly 5 units away from 0. Thus, the absolute value of -5 equals 5, or, in mathematical symbols, $|-5| = 5$. Notice that absolute value is always positive, because it disregards the direction (positive or negative) from which the number approaches 0 on the number line. When you interpret a number in an absolute value sign, just think: Absolutely positive! (Except, of course, for 0, because $|0| = 0$, which is the smallest possible absolute value.)

Note that 5 and -5 are the same distance from 0, which is located halfway between them. In general, if two numbers are opposites of each other, then they have the same absolute value, and 0 is halfway between. If $x = -y$, then you have either of the below:

(You cannot tell which variable is positive and which is negative without more information.)

A Double Negative = A Positive

A double negative occurs when a minus sign is in front of a negative number (which already has its own negative sign). For example:

What is 7 − (−3)?

As you learned in English class, two negatives yield a positive:

$$7 - (-3) = 7 + 3 = 10$$

This is a very easy step to miss, especially when the double negative is somewhat hidden. For example:

What is 7 − (12 − x)?

Many people will make the mistake of computing this as $7 - 12 - x$. However, notice that the second term in the expression in parentheses has a double negative. Therefore, this expression should be simplified as $7 - 12 + x$.

Multiplying & Dividing Signed Numbers

When you multiply or divide numbers, positive or negative, follow one simple rule:

If you have an even number of negative signs, the answer is positive:	$7 \times 8 = 56$ & $(-7) \times (-2) \times 3 = 42$ $56 \div 7 = 8$ & $-42 \div (-7) = 6$
If you have an odd number of negative signs, the answer is negative:	$(-7) \times 8 = -56$ & $7 \times (-2) \times 3 = -42$ $56 \div (-7) = -8$ & $-42 \div 7 = -6$

Try this Data Sufficiency problem:

Is the product of all of the elements in Set S negative?

(1) All of the elements in Set S are negative.
(2) There are 5 negative numbers in Set S.

This is a tricky problem. Based on what you have learned so far, it would seem that statement (2) tells you that the product must be negative. (However, 5 is an odd number, and when the GMAT says "there are 5" of something, you *can* conclude there are *exactly* 5 of that thing.) While it's true that the statement indicates that there are exactly 5 negative numbers in the set, it does not tell you that there are not other numbers in the set. For instance, there could be 5 negative numbers as well as a few other numbers.

If 0 is one of those numbers, then the product will be 0, and 0 is not negative. Therefore, statement (2) is NOT sufficient.

Statement (1) indicates that all of the numbers in the set are negative. If there is an even number of negatives in Set S, the product of these numbers will be positive; if there is an odd number of negatives, the product will be negative. This also is NOT sufficient.

Combined, you know that Set S contains 5 negative numbers and nothing else, so this statement is sufficient. The product of the elements in Set S must be negative. The correct answer is **(C)**.

Disguised Positives & Negatives Questions

Some positives and negatives questions are disguised as inequalities. This generally occurs whenever a question tells you that a quantity is greater than or less than 0, or asks you whether a quantity is greater than or less than 0. For example:

If $\dfrac{a-b}{c} < 0$, is $a > b$?

(1) $c < 0$
(2) $a + b < 0$

The fact that $\dfrac{a-b}{c} < 0$ indicates that $a - b$ and c have *different* signs. That is, one of the expressions is positive and the other is negative.

Therefore, statement (1) establishes that c is negative. Therefore, $a - b$ must be positive:

$$a - b > 0$$
$$a > b$$

Statement (1) is sufficient.

Statement (2) tells you that the sum of a and b is negative. This does not indicate whether a is larger than b, so this statement is NOT sufficient.

The correct answer is **(A)**.

Generally speaking, whenever you see inequalities with the number 0 on either side of the inequality, consider testing positive and negative cases to help solve the problem.

2

The Sum of Two Primes

All prime numbers are odd, except the number 2. (All larger even numbers are divisible by 2, so they cannot be prime.) Thus, the sum of any two primes will be even (odd + odd = even), unless one of those primes is the number 2. So, if you see a sum of two primes that is odd, one of those primes must be the number 2. Conversely, if you know that 2 *cannot* be one of the primes in the sum, then the sum of the two primes must be even. Try an example:

> If a and b are both prime numbers greater than 10, which of the following CANNOT be true?
>
> > I. ab is an even number.
> > II. The difference between a and b equals 117.
> > III. The sum of a and b is even.
>
> (A) I only
> (B) I and II only
> (C) I and III only
> (D) II and III only
> (E) I, II, and III

Since a and b are both prime numbers greater than 10, they must both be odd. Therefore, ab must be an odd number, so statement I cannot be true. Similarly, if a and b are both odd, then $a - b$ cannot equal 117 (an odd number). This difference must be even. Therefore, statement II cannot be true. Finally, since a and b are both odd, $a + b$ must be even, so statement III will always be true. Since statements I and II CANNOT be true, but statement III IS true, the correct answer is **(B)**.

Try the following Data Sufficiency problem:

> If x is an integer greater than 1, what is the value of x?
>
> (1) There are x unique factors of x.
> (2) The sum of x and any prime number larger than x is odd.

Statement (1) indicates that there are x unique factors of x. In order for this to be true, *every* integer between 1 and x, inclusive, must be a factor of x. Try some numbers. This property holds for 1 and for 2, but not for 3 or for 4. In fact, this property does not hold for any higher integer, because no integer x greater than 2 is divisible by $x - 1$. Therefore, x is equal to 1 or 2. However, the question stem indicates that $x > 1$, so x must equal 2. Thus, statement (1) is sufficient.

Statement (2) indicates that x plus any prime number larger than x is odd. Since $x > 1$, x must equal at least 2, so the prime number in question must be larger than 2. Therefore, the prime number is odd. Because the rule is Odd + Even = Odd, then x must be even. However, this is not enough information to indicate the value of x. Therefore, statement (2) is insufficient.

The correct answer is **(A)**.

Problem Set

For questions #1–6, answer each question Odd, Even, or Cannot Be Determined. Try to explain each answer using the rules you learned in this section. All variables in questions #1–6 are assumed to be integers.

1. If $x \div y$ yields an odd integer, what is x?

2. If $a + b$ is even, what is ab?

3. If c, d, and e are consecutive integers, what is cde?

4. If h is even, j is odd, and k is odd, what is $k(h + j)$?

5. If n, p, q, and r are consecutive integers, what is their sum?

6. If xy is even and z is even, what is $x + z$?

7. Simplify $\dfrac{-30}{5} - \dfrac{18 - 9}{-3}$

8. Simplify $\dfrac{20 \times (-7)}{-35 \times (-2)}$

9. If x, y, and z are prime numbers and $x < y < z$, what is the value of x?

    (1) xy is even.
    (2) xz is even.

Save the below problem set for review, either after you finish this book or after you finish all of the Quant books that you plan to study.

10. If c and d are integers, is $c - 3d$ even?

    (1) c and d are odd.
    (2) $c - 2d$ is odd.

11. Is the integer x odd?

    (1) $2(y + x)$ is an odd integer.
    (2) $2y$ is an odd integer.

Solutions

1. **Cannot Be Determined:** There are no guaranteed outcomes in division.

2. **Cannot Be Determined:** If $a + b$ is even, a and b are either both odd or both even. If they are both odd, ab is odd. If they are both even, ab is even.

3. **Even:** At least one of the consecutive integers, c, d, and e, must be even. Therefore, the product cde must be even.

4. **Odd:** $h + j$ must be odd (E + O = O). Therefore, $k(h + j)$ must be odd (O × O = O).

5. **Even:** If n, p, q, and r are consecutive integers, two of them must be odd and two of them must be even. You can pair them up to add them: O + O = E and E + E = E. Adding the pairs, you will see that the sum must be even: E + E = E.

6. **Cannot Be Determined:** If xy is even, then either x or y (or both x and y) must be even. Given that z is even, $x + z$ could be O + E or E + E. Therefore, you cannot determine whether $x + z$ is odd or even.

7. **−3:** This is a two-step subtraction problem. First, simplify each fraction: $\frac{-30}{5} = -6$, and the second fraction simplifies to $\frac{9}{-3}$, which equals −3. The final answer is $-6 - (-3) = -3$.

8. **−2:** The sign of the first product, $20 \times (-7)$, is negative. The sign of the second product, $-35 \times (-2)$, is positive. Therefore, −140 divided by 70 is −2.

9. **(D):** (1) SUFFICIENT: If xy is even, then x is even or y is even. Since $x < y$, x must equal 2, because 2 is the smallest and only even prime number.

(2) SUFFICIENT: Similarly, if xz is even, then x is even or z is even. Since $x < z$, x must equal 2, because 2 is the smallest and only even prime number.

10. **(A):** (1) SUFFICIENT: If both c and d are odd, then $c - 3d$ equals O − (3 × O) = O − O = E.

(2) INSUFFICIENT: If $c - 2d$ is odd, then c must be odd, because $2d$ will always be even. However, this tells you nothing about d.

Therefore, the correct answer is **(A)**.

11. **(E):** (1) INSUFFICIENT: $2(y + x)$ is an odd integer. How is it possible that 2 multipled by something could yield an odd integer? The value in the parentheses must not be an integer itself. For example, the decimal 1.5 times 2 yields the odd integer 3. List some other possibilities:

$$2(y + x) = 1, 3, 5, 7, 9, \text{etc.}$$
$$(y + x) = \frac{1}{2}, \frac{3}{2}, \frac{5}{2}, \frac{7}{2}, \frac{9}{2}, \text{etc.}$$

You know that x is an integer, so y must be a fraction in order to get such a fractional sum. Say that $y = \frac{1}{2}$. In that case, $x = 0, 1, 2, 3, 4$, etc. Thus, x can be either odd ("yes") or even ("no").

(2) INSUFFICIENT: This statement tells you nothing about x. If $2y$ is an odd integer, this implies that $y = \dfrac{\text{odd}}{2} = \dfrac{1}{2}, \dfrac{3}{2}, \dfrac{5}{2}$, etc.

(1) AND (2) INSUFFICIENT: Statement (2) fails to eliminate the case you used in statement (1) to determine that x can be either odd or even. Thus, you still cannot answer the question with a definite yes or no.

But, just to combine the statements another way:

Statement (1) says that $2(y + x) = 2y + 2x =$ an odd integer.
Statement (2) says that $2y =$ an odd integer. By substitution, odd $+ 2x =$ odd, so $2x =$ odd $-$ odd $=$ even. $2x$ would be even regardless of whether x is even or odd.

The correct answer is **(E)**.

Chapter 3
of
Number Properties

Strategy: Test Cases

In This Chapter...

Chapter 3

Strategy: Test Cases

Certain problems allow for multiple possible scenarios, or cases. When you **test cases**, you try different numbers in a problem to see whether you have the same outcome or different outcomes.

The strategy plays out a bit differently for Data Sufficiency (DS) than for Problem Solving (PS); both will be covered in this chapter. (If you have not yet studied Data Sufficiency, please see Appendix A.)

Try this problem, using any solution method you like:

> Is integer x odd?
>
> (1) $2x + 1$ is odd.
> (2) $\dfrac{x}{2}$ is even.

How to Test Cases

Here's how to test cases to solve the above problem:

Step 1: What possible cases are allowed?

The problem indicates that x is an integer; it could be positive, negative, or the number 0, but it is not a fraction (or decimal).

Step 2: Choose numbers that work for the statement.

Before you dive into the work, remember this crucial rule:

> When choosing numbers to test cases, ONLY choose numbers that are allowed by that statement.

If you inadvertently choose numbers that make the statement false, discard that case and try again.

Step 3: Try to prove the statement *insufficient*.

Here's how:

(1) $2x + 1$ is odd.

What numbers would make this statement true?

Case 1: $x = 6$.

Statement true? $2x + 1$ is odd.	Is x odd?
$2(6) + 1 = 13$ ✓	No

First, ensure that the value you've chosen does make the statement true. In this case, plugging in 6 for x does produce an odd result, so $x = 6$ is a valid number to test.

Second, answer the question asked. If $x = 6$, then x is not odd.

Next, ask yourself: Is there another case that would make the statement true but give you a *different* outcome?

Case 2: $x = 3$.

Statement true? $2x + 1$ is odd.	Is x odd?
$2(3) + 1 = 7$ ✓	Yes

Because x could be odd or even, this statement is NOT sufficient to answer the question; ~~AD~~ cross off answers (A) and (D). Try statement (2) next. Whenever possible, reuse the num- BCE bers that you tried for the first statement.

(2) $\dfrac{x}{2}$ is even.

Case 1: $x = 6$.

Statement true? $\left(\dfrac{x}{2} \text{ is even}\right)$	Is x odd?
$\dfrac{6}{2} = 3$ ✗	

Careful! The result is not even; it's odd. You have to pick a value that makes statement (2) true. Discard this case. (Literally cross it off on your scrap paper.)

What kind of number will make statement (2) true?

Case 2: $x = 8$.

Statement true? $\left(\dfrac{x}{2} \text{ is even}\right)$	Is x odd?
$\dfrac{8}{2} = 4$ ✓	No

You've got a "no" answer. Can you think of a value that would return a "yes" answer?

Case 3: $x = 3$.

Statement true? $\left(\dfrac{x}{2} \text{ is even}\right)$	Is x odd?
$\dfrac{3}{2} = 1.5$ ✗	

Nope, that won't work either. In fact, you can't divide an odd number by 2 and get an integer result. Therefore, no odd number will ever make statement (2) true.

In other words, this statement only allows even numbers. You can answer the question: Is x odd? No, never.

~~AD~~
ⒷCE

The correct answer is **(B)**.

When you test cases in Data Sufficiency, your ultimate goal is to try to prove the statement insufficient, if you can. The first case you try will give you one outcome. For the next case, think about what numbers would be likely to give you a *different* outcome.

As soon as you do find two different outcomes, as in statement (1) above, you know the statement is not sufficient, and you can cross off some answer choices and move on.

If you cannot find two different outcomes, then you may be able to prove to yourself why you will always get the same outcome, as in statement (2) above. If you have tried several times to prove the statement insufficient but you keep getting the same outcome, then that statement is probably sufficient.

Try a Problem Solving example:

If $ab > 0$, which of the following must be negative?

(A) $a + b$ (B) $|a| + b$ (C) $b - a$ (D) $\dfrac{a}{b}$ (E) $-\dfrac{a}{b}$

Step 1: **What possible cases are allowed?**
On Problem Solving problems, *must be* or *could be* language is a signal that you can test cases.

When you see > 0 (or < 0), know that you've got a positive/negative problem in disguise. In this case, if the product of the two variables is positive, then a and b must have the same sign: either both are positive or both are negative.

Step 2: **Choose numbers that work for the given information.**
On DS problems, your task is to choose numbers that are valid for the given statements. On PS problems, your task is to choose numbers that are valid for any given information. In this case, you can only choose values that make $ab > 0$.

Step 3: **Try to prove each answer choice *wrong*.**
The question asks which answer must be negative. If you can find one circumstance in which a particular answer choice is *not* negative, then you can cross that answer off.

Test each answer choice, using a chart to keep track of your work. Take the time to write out each answer; if you work off of the screen, you're much more likely to make a careless mistake. As soon as you find a positive or 0 scenario, cross off that answer and move to the next row.

Answer	$a = 2, b = 1$	$a = -1, b = -2$	
(A) $a + b$	$2 + 1 = 3$		Eliminate.
(B) $|a| + b$	$2 + 1 = 3$		Eliminate.
(C) $b - a$	$1 - 2 = -1$	$-2 - (-1) = -1$	
(D) $\dfrac{a}{b}$	$\dfrac{2}{1}$		Eliminate.
(E) $-\dfrac{a}{b}$	$-\dfrac{2}{1}$	$-\left(\dfrac{-1}{-2}\right) = -\dfrac{1}{2}$	

Three wrong answers down, one more to go. As you're testing the cases, you may realize that if you change the numbers just a bit, you'll get a different response. If that's the case, feel free to test a different set of numbers right away; you don't have to get through all five answer choices first.

MANHATTAN
PREP

In this case, if you flip around the values ($a = 1$, $b = 2$), then answer (C) turns positive; eliminate it.

The correct answer is **(E)**. If $ab > 0$, then $\dfrac{a}{b}$ also has to be greater than 0. Adding a negative sign to a positive number will always turn it negative.

To sum up, when you are asked to test cases, follow three main steps:

Step 1: What possible cases are allowed?

Before you start solving, make sure you know what restrictions have been placed on the basic problem in the question stem. You may be told that the particular number is positive, or odd, and so on. Follow these restrictions when choosing numbers to test.

Step 2: Choose numbers that work for the given information.

Pause for a moment to remind yourself that you are only allowed to choose numbers that are valid for the given information in that problem. On both PS and DS problems, the question stem may contain givens. On DS problems, the statements are always givens.

With enough practice, this will become second nature. If you answer a testing cases problem incorrectly but aren't sure why, see whether you accidentally tested cases that weren't allowed because they weren't valid options for the statement or given information.

Step 3: Try to prove the statement *insufficient* or the answer wrong.

On DS questions, when the problem discusses abstract characteristics rather than real numbers, test cases to try to prove the statement insufficient:

Value

Sufficient: single numerical answer

Insufficient: two or more possible answers

Yes/No

Sufficient: Always Yes *or* Always No

Insufficient: Maybe or Sometimes Yes, Sometimes No

On PS questions, look for *must be* or *could be* language, such as:

- What must be true?
- What could be true?
- Which of the following must be even?
- Which of the following could equal 5?

This language will be your signal to try to disprove the four wrong answers.

The Theory Shortcut

The last problem can also be solved using a more theoretical approach, as long as you feel very comfortable with the concepts being tested. For example:

> If $ab > 0$, which of the following must be negative?
>
> (A) $a + b$ (B) $|a| + b$ (C) $b - a$ (D) $\dfrac{a}{b}$ (E) $-\dfrac{a}{b}$

As always, your goal is to try to prove the answers wrong. When you find a positive or 0 scenario, cross off that answer immediately. Think your way through each answer using your knowledge of positive and negative rules:

Answer	$a +, b +$	
(A) $a + b$	+	If a and b are +, the sum is +.
(B) $|a| + b$	+	Both are +, so the sum is +.
(C) $b - a$	can be +	As long as b is larger, the difference will be +. But if b is smaller, it will be −.
(D) $\dfrac{a}{b}$	+	If product is +, so is quotient.
(E) $-\dfrac{a}{b}$	−	If product is +, so is quotient. Adding a − sign makes this one always −.

Try the theory approach on this problem:

> Is $pqr > 0$?
>
> (1) $pq > 0$
>
> (2) $\dfrac{q}{r} < 0$

The problem asks about characteristics of numbers in general; it doesn't ask about specific numbers. Time to test some cases!

Step 1: What possible cases are allowed?

Is $pqr > 0$?

The question stem does not contain any restrictions. The numbers can be positive, negative, fractions, or 0—anything goes.

Note that the question stem does ask whether the product is greater than 0. A quick glance at the statements confirms that they contain similar information. This is a positive/negative question.

Before trying numbers, think about what would need to be true to answer yes vs. no. Use a table to keep track of your thinking:

p	q	r	$pqr > 0$?
+	+	+	Yes
+	−	−	Yes
+	+	−	No
−	−	−	No
0	+	−	No

Yes if any 2 are negative

No if any 1 is negative

No if all 3 are negative

No if any are 0

Step 2: **Choose numbers that work for the given statements.**

Step 3: **Try to prove the statements _insufficient_.**

(1) $pq > 0$

p	q	$pq > 0$?	$pqr > 0$?
+	+	Yes	Maybe

Depends on r

If r is positive, then the product is positive, but if r is negative, then the product is negative. This statement is insufficient.

(2) $\dfrac{q}{r} < 0$

q	r	$\dfrac{q}{r} < 0$?	$pqr > 0$?
+	−	Yes	Maybe

Depends on p

If p is positive, then the product is negative. If p is negative, then the product is positive. This statement is insufficient.

Try the two statements together:

(1) $pq > 0$

(2) $\dfrac{q}{r} < 0$

p	q	r	Statements true?	$pqr > 0$?
+	+	−	Yes	No
−	−	+	Yes	Yes

If p is positive, then q must also be positive and r must be negative. In this case, pqr is less than 0.

On the other hand, if *p* is negative, then *q* must also be negative and *r* must be positive. In this case, *pqr* is greater than 0.

Even when used together, the two statements are insufficient to answer the question. The correct answer is **(E)**.

Often, you'll test cases using numbers all the way through. At times, though, you'll be able to use the real numbers you're testing to uncover the underlying theory tested by the problem. You can use this theory to shortcut the process a bit and arrive at your answer more quickly—just be sure that you really do understand the theoretical approach. If you're not 100% sure, don't use the shortcut. Test real numbers instead.

When to Test Cases

You can test cases whenever a problem allows multiple possible scenarios rather than just one numerical outcome. In that case, try some of the different possibilities allowed in order to see whether different scenarios, or cases, result in different outcomes or in the same outcome.

When testing cases, your initial starting point is every possible number on the number line. However, many problems give you restrictions that narrow the possible values, such as specifying that a number has to be an integer, or less than 0, or even. Write down your restrictions before you begin testing cases.

Think about different classes of numbers that are commonly tested on the GMAT. For example:

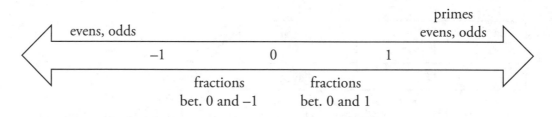

Problems will include clues that can help you decide which numbers to test. If a problem mentions a specific characteristic, such as odd, then of course try odds and evens. If an absolute value symbol appears, try negatives. If exponents come into play, try 0, 1, and fractions between 0 and 1 (these numbers do funny things when squared!). Picture the number line (or draw it out) and try any categories allowed by the givens that you think might make the difference in proving a DS statement insufficient or eliminating a PS answer.

How to Get Better at Testing Cases

First, practice the problems at the end of this chapter and in your OG problem sets online. Try each problem using the three-step process for testing cases. If you mess up any part of the process, try the problem again, making sure to write out all of your work.

Afterwards, review the problem. In particular, see whether you can articulate the reason why certain statements are sufficient (as the solutions to the earlier problems did). Could you explain those statements to a fellow student who is confused? If so, then you are starting to learn both the process by which you test cases and the underlying principles that these kinds of problems test.

If not, then look up the solution in this book or in GMAT Navigator™, search online, or ask an instructor or fellow student for help.

3

Problem Set

It's time to test out your testing cases skills. Both of these problems can be answered by testing cases.

1. If x is a positive integer, is $x^2 + 6x + 10$ odd?

    (1) $x^2 + 4x + 5$ is odd.
    (2) $x^2 + 3x + 4$ is even.

2. If p, q, and r are integers, is $pq + r$ even?

    (1) $p + r$ is even.
    (2) $q + r$ is odd.

3

Solutions

1. **(A):** The question can first be simplified by noting that if x is even, $x^2 + 6x + 10$ will be even, and if x is odd, $x^2 + 6x + 10$ will be odd.

Thus, you can simplify this question: "Is x odd or even?"

(A couple of shortcuts to save time in reaching that conclusion: the exponent on the first term can be ignored, since an even squared is still even and an odd squared is still odd. You know $6x$ will be even no matter what, since 6 is even, and obviously 10 is even no matter what. So, an even plus two evens is even, and an odd plus two evens is odd.)

(1) SUFFICIENT: You can test odd and even cases or simply use number theory. If x is even, you get even + even + odd = odd, and if x is odd, you get odd + even + odd = even. Thus, since $x^2 + 4x + 5$ is odd, x is even.

(2) INSUFFICIENT: $x^2 + 3x + 4$ is actually even regardless of what integer is plugged in for x. If x is even, you get even + even + even = even, and if x is odd, you get odd + odd + even = even. Thus, x could be odd or even. Plugging in numbers will yield the same conclusion—x could be any integer.

Note that you should *not* factor any of the expressions above. If you wasted time factoring, remember: factoring is meaningless if you don't have an equation set equal to 0! This problem was about number theory (or number testing), not factoring.

The correct answer is **(A)**.

2. **(E):** The yes/no question asks whether $pq + r$ is even. What would need to be true in order for the answer to be yes? Either both pq and r need to be even or both pq and r need to be odd.

(1) INSUFFICIENT: You are told that $p + r$ is even. To stay organized, test all the cases that make the statement true. Both p and r are even, or both p and r are odd. For each of those scenarios, q could be odd or even. Set up a table to keep track of all of these possibilities:

Scenario	p	q	r	$pq + r$
1	Odd	Odd	Odd	O × O + O = E
2	Odd	Even	Odd	O × E + O = O
3	Even	Odd	Even	E × O + E = E
4	Even	Even	Even	E × E + E = E

Since $pq + r$ could be odd or even, statement (1) is not sufficient. Note that you can stop as soon as you have found contradictory cases (one odd and one even); above, for example, you could have stopped after Scenario 2.

(2) INSUFFICIENT: As in statement (1), you can organize the information from statement (2) with a table. Either q is even and r is odd or q is odd and r is even, and p can be odd or even:

Scenario	p	q	r	$pq + r$
5	Odd	Even	Odd	O × E + O = O
6	Even	Even	Odd	E × E + O = O
7	Odd	Odd	Even	O × O + E = O
8	Even	Odd	Even	E × O + E = E

(1) AND (2) INSUFFICIENT: Notice that Scenarios 2 and 5 are identical, as are Scenarios 3 and 8. Therefore, both sets of scenarios meet the criteria laid forth in statements (1) and (2), but they yield opposite answers to the question:

Scenario	p	q	r	$pq + r$
2 & 5	Odd	Even	Odd	O × E + O = O
3 & 8	Even	Odd	Even	E × O + E = E

The correct answer is **(E)**.

Chapter 4

Combinatorics

In This Chapter...

Chapter 4
Combinatorics

The Words "OR" and "AND"

Suppose you are at a restaurant that offers a free side dish of soup or salad with any main dish. How many possible side dishes can you order?

You have two options: the soup OR the salad. This is a straightforward example, but it demonstrates an important principle: the word *or* means *add*. You will see this word show up again and again in both combinatorics and probability problems.

Now let's complicate the situation a bit. The same restaurant has three main dishes: steak, chicken, and salmon. How many possible combinations of main dish and side dish are there?

Now there are two decisions that need to be made. A diner must select a main dish AND a side dish. You can list out all the possible combinations:

Steak – Soup	Chicken – Soup	Salmon – Soup
Steak – Salad	Chicken – Salad	Salmon – Salad

There are six possible combinations. Fortunately, there is a way to avoid listing out every single combination. This brings us to the second important principle of combinatorics: the word *and* means *multiply*.

When you make two decisions, you make decision 1 AND decision 2. This is true whether the decisions are simultaneous (e.g., choosing a main dish and a side dish) or sequential (e.g., choosing among routes between successive towns on a road trip).

In this example, you have 3 options for main dishes AND 2 options for side dishes, so you have $3 \times 2 = 6$ options.

Believe it or not, the principles of combinatorics are derived from these two simple principles:

1. OR means *add*.

2. AND means *multiply*.

For instance, one way of interpreting the previous example is:

(steak OR chicken OR salmon)　　AND　(soup OR salad)
(　1 　+ 　 1 　 + 　 1 　)　 × 　(1 　+ 　1 　)　 = 　 6
　　　　　　　3　　　　　　　　×　　　　2　　　 = 　 6

Unfortunately, questions will not always use the words *and* and *or* directly. Try the following example:

> An office manager must choose a five-digit lock code for the office door. The first
> and last digits of the code must be odd, and no repetition of digits is allowed.
> How many different lock codes are possible?

The question "How many ... ?" usually signals a combinatorics problem. If the manager has to pick a five-digit lock code, he has to make five decisions. To keep track, make a slot for each digit:

_____ × _____ × _____ × _____ × _____
Digit 1　AND　Digit 2　AND　Digit 3　AND　Digit 4　AND　Digit 5

Next, fill in the number of options for each slot. This is known as the **slot method**.

How many options are there for each digit? Be careful; there are restrictions on the first and last number. Start with the most constrained decisions first.

The first digit can be 1 OR 3 OR 5 OR 7 OR 9. There are 5 options for the first digit. Remember, there can be no repeated numbers. Now that you have chosen the first digit (even though you don't know which one it is) there are only 4 odd numbers remaining for the last digit.

___5___ × _____ × _____ × _____ × ___4___
Digit 1　AND　Digit 2　AND　Digit 3　AND　Digit 4　AND　Digit 5

Now, fill in the rest of the slots. Make sure to account for the lack of repetition. Ten digits exist in total (0 through 9), but two have already been used, so there are 8 options for the 2nd digit, 7 options for the 3rd digit, and 6 options for the 4th digit:

___5___ × ___8___ × ___7___ × ___6___ × ___4___ = 6,720
Digit 1　AND　Digit 2　AND　Digit 3　AND　Digit 4　AND　Digit 5

Any time a question involves making decisions, there are two cases:

1. Decision 1 OR Decision 2 (add possibilities)
2. Decision 1 AND Decision 2 (multiply possibilities)

Arranging Groups

Another very common type of combinatorics problem asks how many different ways there are to arrange a group.

The number of ways of arranging n distinct objects, if there are no restrictions, is $n!$ (n factorial).

The term "n factorial" ($n!$) refers to the product of all the integers from 1 to n, inclusive. If you would like an 80th percentile or higher score on the Quant section of the GMAT, memorize the first six factorials:

$1! = 1$ $4! = 4 \times 3 \times 2 \times 1 = 24$

$2! = 2 \times 1 = 2$ $5! = 5 \times 4 \times 3 \times 2 \times 1 = 120$

$3! = 3 \times 2 \times 1 = 6$ $6! = 6 \times 5 \times 4 \times 3 \times 2 \times 1 = 720$

For example, how many ways are there to arrange 4 people in 4 chairs in a row? Using the **slot method**, there is one slot for each position in the row. If you place any one of 4 people in the first chair, then you can place any one of the remaining 3 people in the second chair. For the third and fourth chairs you have 2 choices and then 1 choice.

$$\underline{\quad 4 \quad} \times \underline{\quad 3 \quad} \times \underline{\quad 2 \quad} \times \underline{\quad 1 \quad} = 24 \text{ arrangements}$$

Once you understand what the formula means, you can just say "the number of ways to arrange 4 people equals 4 factorial, which equals 24."

Arranging Groups Using the Anagram Grid

More complicated problems can be solved using the **anagram grid**.

For example, how many arrangements are there of the letters in the word "EEL"?

There are 3 letters, so according to the factorial formula, there should be $3! = 6$ arrangements. But because two of the letters are the same, there are only 3 arrangements:

EEL   ELE   LEE

If you put subscripts on the two "E"s, you can see where the other arrangements went:

E_1E_2L E_1LE_2 LE_1E_2

E_2E_1L E_2LE_1 LE_2E_1

The two arrangements in each column are considered identical. Each pair of arrangements counts as one.

Try the following problem:

> Seven people enter a race. There are 4 types of medals given as prizes for completing the race. The winner gets a platinum medal, the runner-up gets a gold medal, the next two racers each get a silver medal, and the last 3 racers all get bronze medals. What is the number of different ways the medals can be awarded?

In order to keep track of all the different categories, create an **anagram grid**. Anagram grids can be used whenever you are arranging members of a group.

The number of columns in the grid will always be equal to the number of members of the group. There are 7 runners in the race, so there should be 7 columns. Next, categorize each member of the group. There are 1 platinum medal, 1 gold medal, 2 silver medals, and 3 bronze medals. Note: use only letters for the bottom row, never numbers (you'll see why in a minute).

1	2	3	4	5	6	7
P	G	S	S	B	B	B

Just as the two E's in "EEL" were indistinguishable, the 2 silver medals and the 3 bronze medals are indistinguishable, so the answer is not 7!. Use the top and bottom rows to create a fraction:

$$\frac{7!}{1!1!2!3!}$$

The numerator of the fraction is the factorial of the largest number in the top row, in this case 7!. The denominator is the product of the factorials of each *different* kind of letter in the bottom row. In this case, there are one P, one G, two S's, and three B's. (Use only letters, not numbers, in the bottom row to avoid mixing up the number of repeats with the numbers themselves.)

The above graphic shows the 1! terms for both P and G, but in practice, you don't have to write out any 1! terms, since they don't make a difference to the calculation. As you simplify the fraction, look for ways to cancel out numbers in the denominator with numbers in the numerator:

$$\frac{7!}{3!2!} = \frac{7\times6\times5\times\cancel{4}^2\times\cancel{3!}}{_1\cancel{2}\times1\times\cancel{3!}} = 7\times6\times5\times2 = 420$$

Try another problem:

> A local card club will send 3 representatives to the national conference. If the local club has 8 members, how many different groups of representatives could the club send?

The problem talks about 8 members, so draw 8 columns for the anagram grid. There are 3 representatives chosen; represent them with Y. Use N to represent the 5 members of the group who are not chosen.

1	2	3	4	5	6	7	8
Y	Y	Y	N	N	N	N	N

Set up your fraction:

$$\frac{8!}{3!5!} = \frac{8 \times 7 \times \cancel{6}^{\,3} \times \cancel{5!}}{(_1\cancel{3} \times _1\cancel{2} \times 1)\cancel{5!}} = 8 \times 7 = 56$$

Don't write out all of the numbers on the top of the fraction; only write out the numbers down to the largest factorial on the bottom of the fraction. In the above case, you can cancel out the two 5! terms without having to write them out.

Multiple Groups

So far, the discussion has revolved around two main themes: (1) making decisions, and (2) arranging groups. Difficult combinatorics questions will actually combine the two topics. In other words, you may have to make multiple decisions, each of which will involve arranging different groups.

Try the following problem:

> The I Eta Pi fraternity must choose a delegation of 3 senior members and 2 junior members for an annual interfraternity conference. If I Eta Pi has 6 senior members and 5 junior members, how many different delegations are possible?

First, note that you are choosing senior members AND junior members. These are different decisions, so you need to determine each separately and then multiply the possible arrangements.

You have to pick 3 seniors out of a group of 6. That means that 3 are chosen (and identical) and the remaining 3 are not chosen (and also identical):

$$\frac{6!}{3!3!} = \frac{_{\cancel{3}}\cancel{6} \times 5 \times 4 \times \cancel{3!}}{(_1\cancel{3} \times _1\cancel{2} \times 1)\cancel{3!}} = 5 \times 4 = 20$$

Similarly, you need to pick 2 juniors out of a group of 5; 2 members are chosen (and identical) and the remaining 3 members are not chosen (and also identical):

$$\frac{5!}{2!3!} = \frac{5 \times \cancel{4}^2 \times \cancel{3!}}{(\cancel{2} \times 1)\cancel{3!}} = 5 \times 2 = 10$$

There are 20 possible senior delegations AND 10 possible junior delegations. Remember, AND means multiply. Together there are 20 × 10 = 200 possible delegations.

Questions will not always make it clear that you are dealing with multiple decisions. Try the following problem:

> The yearbook committee has to pick a color scheme for this year's yearbook. There are 7 colors to choose from (red, orange, yellow, green, blue, indigo, and violet). How many different color schemes are possible if the committee can select at most 2 colors?

Although this question concerns only one group (colors), it also involves multiple decisions. Notice the question states there can be *at most* 2 colors chosen. That means the color scheme can contain 1 color OR 2 colors.

Figure out how many combinations are possible if 1 color is chosen and if 2 colors are chosen, and then add them together:

$$1 \text{ color chosen and 6 colors not chosen} = \frac{7!}{1!6!} = 7$$
$$2 \text{ colors chosen and 5 colors not chosen} = \frac{7!}{2!5!} = 21$$

Together there are 7 plus 21, or 28, possible color schemes.

Problem Set

1. In how many different ways can the letters in the word "LEVEL" be arranged?

2. Amy and Adam are making boxes of truffles to give out as wedding favors. They have an unlimited supply of 5 different types of truffles. If each box holds 2 truffles of different types, how many different boxes can they make?

3. A pod of 6 dolphins always swims single file, with 3 females at the front and 3 males in the rear. In how many different arrangements can the dolphins swim?

Save the below problems for review, either after you finish this book or after you finish all of the Quant books that you plan to study.

4. Mario's Pizza has 2 choices of crust: deep dish and thin-and-crispy. The restaurant also has a choice of 5 toppings: tomatoes, sausage, peppers, onions, and pepperoni. Finally, Mario's offers every pizza in extra cheese as well as regular. If Linda's volleyball team decides to order a pizza with 4 toppings, how many different choices do the teammates have at Mario's Pizza?

5. What is the sum of all the possible three-digit numbers that can be constructed using the digits 3, 4, and 5 if each digit can be used only once in each number?

Solutions

1. **30 ways:** There are two repeated E's and two repeated L's in the word "LEVEL." To find the anagrams for this word, set up a fraction in which the numerator is the factorial of the number of letters and the denominator is the factorial of the number of each repeated letter:

$$\frac{5!}{2!2!} = \frac{5 \times 4 \times 3 \times 2 \times 1}{2 \times 1 \times 2 \times 1} = 30$$

Alternatively, you can solve this problem using the slot method, as long as you correct for over-counting (since you have some indistinguishable elements). There are 5 choices for the first letter, 4 for the second, and so on, making the product $5 \times 4 \times 3 \times 2 \times 1 = 120$. However, there are two sets of 2 indistinguishable elements each, so you must divide by 2! to account for each of these. Thus, the total number of combinations is $\frac{5 \times 4 \times 3 \times 2 \times 1}{2! \times 2!} = 30$.

2. **10 boxes:** In every combination, 2 types of truffles will be in the box, and 3 types of truffles will not. Therefore, this problem is a question about the number of anagrams that can be made from the "word" YYNNN:

$$\frac{5!}{2!3!} = \frac{5 \times 4 \times 3 \times 2 \times 1}{3 \times 2 \times 1 \times 2 \times 1} = 5 \times 2 = 10$$

A	B	C	D	E
Y	Y	N	N	N

3. **36 arrangements:** There are 3! ways in which the 3 females can swim. There are 3! ways in which the 3 males can swim. Therefore, there are 3! × 3! ways in which the entire pod can swim:

$$3! \times 3! = 6 \times 6 = 36$$

This is a multiple arrangements problem, in which you have 2 separate pools (females and males).

4. **20 choices:** Consider the toppings first. Model the toppings with the "word" YYYYN, in which four of the toppings are on the pizza and one is not. The number of anagrams for this "word" is:

$$\frac{5!}{4!} = 5$$

A	B	C	D	E
Y	Y	Y	Y	N

If each of these pizzas can also be offered in 2 choices of crust, there are $5 \times 2 = 10$ pizzas. The same logic applies for extra cheese and regular: $10 \times 2 = 20$.

5. **2,664:** There are 6 ways in which to arrange these digits: 345, 354, 435, 453, 534, and 543. Notice that each digit appears twice in the hundreds column, twice in the tens column, and twice in the ones column. Therefore, you can use your knowledge of place value to find the sum quickly. Because each digit appears twice in the hundreds column, you have $3 + 3 + 4 + 4 + 5 + 5 = 24$ in the hundreds column. If you multiply 24 by 100, you get the value of all of the numbers in that column. Repeat this reasoning for the tens column and the ones column:

$$100(24) + 10(24) + (24) = 2,400 + 240 + 24 = 2,664$$

Chapter 5 of Number Properties

Probability

In This Chapter...

Chapter 5
Probability

Probability is a quantity that expresses the chance, or likelihood, of an event.

Think of probability as a fraction:

$$\text{Probability} = \frac{\text{Number of } desired \text{ or } successful \text{ outcomes}}{\text{Total number of } possible \text{ outcomes}}$$

For instance, if you flip a coin, the probability that heads turns up is $\frac{1}{2}$. There were two possible outcomes (heads or tails), but only one of them is considered desirable (heads).

Notice that the numerator of the fraction is *always* a subset of the denominator. If there are n possible outcomes, then the number of desirable outcomes must be between 0 and n (the number of outcomes cannot be negative). Simply put, *any probability will be between 0 and 1*. An impossible event has a probability of 0; a certain event has a probability of 1.

Additionally, you may be required to express probability as a fraction, a decimal, or a percent. For instance, $\frac{3}{4} = 0.75 = 75\%$. Although a question may ask for a probability in any one of these forms, you will first need to think of it as a fraction in order to make the necessary calculations.

Calculate the Numerator and Denominator Separately

Numerators and denominators of probabilities are related, but they must be calculated separately. Often, it will be easier to begin by calculating the denominator.

There are two ways to calculate a number of outcomes for either the numerator or the denominator:

1. Use an appropriate combinatorics formula.
2. Manually count the number of outcomes.

Try the following problem:

> Two number cubes with faces numbered 1 to 6 are rolled. What is the probability that the sum of the rolls is 8?

Start with the total number of possible outcomes (the denominator). For this calculation you can use combinatorics. Notice that rolling two number cubes is like rolling cube 1 AND rolling cube 2. For each of these rolls, there are 6 possible outcomes (the numbers 1 to 6). Since AND equals multiply, there are $6 \times 6 = 36$ possible outcomes. This is the denominator of your fraction.

Next, figure out how many of those 36 possible rolls represent the desired outcome (a sum of 8). Can you think of an appropriate combinatorics formula? Probably not. Truth be told, the writers of this guide can't think of a formula either.

Fortunately, you don't need a formula. Only a limited number of combinations would work. Count them up! When you *have to* count, you never have to count too much. If the first die turns up a 1, the other die would need to roll a 7. This isn't possible, so eliminate that possibility. Keep counting; here are the rolls that work:

$$2-6 \quad 3-5 \quad 4-4 \quad 5-3 \quad 6-2$$

That's it; there are 5 combinations that work. Therefore, the probability of a sum of 8 is $\frac{5}{36}$.

More Than One Event: "AND" vs. "OR"

Combinatorics and probability have another connection: the meaning of the words AND and OR. In probability, as well as in combinatorics, the word AND means multiply and the word OR means add.

> There is a $\frac{1}{2}$ probability that a certain coin will turn up heads on any given toss.
> What is the probability that two tosses of the coin will yield heads both times?

To answer this question, calculate the probability that the coin lands on heads on the first flip AND heads on the second flip. The probability of heads on the first flip is $\frac{1}{2}$. The probability of heads on the second flip is also $\frac{1}{2}$. Since AND means multiply, the probability is $\frac{1}{2} \times \frac{1}{2} = \frac{1}{4}$.

Try another example:

> The weather report for today states that there is a 40% chance of sun, a 25% chance of rain, and a 35% chance of hail. Assuming only one of the three outcomes can happen, what is the probability that it rains or hails today?

The question is asking for the probability of rain OR hail. Therefore, the probability is 25% + 35% = 60%. The calculation would change if *both* rain and hail can happen, but don't worry about that for now.

P(A) + P(Not A) = 1

P(A) + P(Not A) = 1 is really just a fancy way of saying that the probability of something happening plus the probability of that thing *not* happening must sum to 1. For example, the probability that it rains or doesn't rain equals 1: if there's a 25% chance of rain, then there must be a 75% chance that it will *not* rain. Try an example:

> A person has a 40% chance of winning a game every time he or she plays it. If there are no ties, what is the probability that Asha loses the game the first time she plays and wins the second time she plays?

If the probability of winning the game is 40%, then the odds of *not* winning the game (losing) are 100% − 40% = 60%. Calculate the odds that Asha loses the game the first time AND wins the game the second time:

$$(60\%) \times (40\%) = 0.6 \times 0.4 = 0.24$$

The probability is 0.24, or 24%.

The 1 − x Probability Trick

Suppose that a salesperson makes 5 sales calls, and you want to find the likelihood that he or she makes *at least 1* sale. If you try to calculate this probability directly, you will have to confront 5 separate possibilities that constitute "success": exactly 1 sale, exactly 2 sales, exactly 3 sales, exactly 4 sales, or exactly 5 sales. This would almost certainly be more work than you can reasonably do in two minutes.

There is, however, another option. Instead of calculating the probability that the salesperson makes at least one sale, you can calculate the probability that the salesperson does *not* make at least one sale. Then, you could subtract that probability from 1. This shortcut works because the thing that does *not* happen represents a smaller number of the possible outcomes: that is, *not* getting at least 1 sale is the same thing as getting 0 sales, which is just one of the total possible outcomes. By contrast, making at least 1 sale represents 5 separate possible outcomes. When this occurs, it is much easier to calculate the probability for that one possible outcome (0 sales) and then subtract from 1.

For complicated probability problems, decide whether it is easier to calculate the probability you want or the probability you do *not* want. Try an example:

> A bag contains equal numbers of red, green, and yellow marbles. If Geeta pulls three marbles out of the bag, replacing each marble after she picks it, what is the probability that at least one will be red?

The quick way to answer this question is to calculate the probability that *none* of the marbles are red. For each of the three picks, there is a $\frac{2}{3}$ probability that the marble will not be red. The probability that all three marbles will not be red is $\frac{2}{3} \times \frac{2}{3} \times \frac{2}{3} = \frac{8}{27}$.

If the probability that *none* of the marbles is red is $\frac{8}{27}$, then the probability that at least one marble is red is $1 - \frac{8}{27} = \frac{19}{27}$.

If you need to calculate the probability of an event (P(A)), there are two ways to calculate the probability:

P(A)   or   1 – P(Not A)

When the question includes *at least* or *at most* language, the 1 – P(Not A) method is usually faster.

Problem Set

For problems #1 and #2, assume that each number cube has 6 sides with faces numbered 1 to 6.

1. What is the probability that the sum of two number cubes will yield a 10 or lower?

2. What is the probability that the sum of two number cubes will yield a 7, and then when both are thrown again, their sum will again yield a 7?

3. There is a 30% chance of rain and a 70% chance of shine. If it rains, there is a 50% chance that Bob will cancel his picnic, but if the sun is shining, he will definitely have his picnic. What is the chance that Bob will have his picnic?

Save the below problem set for review, either after you finish this book or after you finish all of the Quant books that you plan to study.

4. In a diving competition, each diver has a 20% chance of a perfect dive. The first perfect dive of the competition, but no subsequent dives, will receive a perfect score. If Janet is the third diver to dive, what is her chance of receiving a perfect score? (Assume that each diver can perform only one dive per turn.)

5. A magician has five animals in his magic hat: 3 doves and 2 rabbits. If he pulls two animals out of the hat at random, what is the chance that he will have a matched pair?

5

Solutions

1. $\dfrac{11}{12}$: Solve this problem by calculating the probability that the sum will be higher than 10 and sub-tracting the result from 1. There are 3 combinations of 2 number cubes that yield a sum higher than 10: $5 + 6$, $6 + 5$, and $6 + 6$. Therefore, the probability that the sum will be higher than 10 is $\dfrac{3}{36}$, or $\dfrac{1}{12}$. The probability that the sum will be 10 or lower is $1 - \dfrac{1}{12} = \dfrac{11}{12}$.

2. $\dfrac{1}{36}$: There are 36 ways in which 2 number cubes can be thrown ($6 \times 6 = 36$). The combinations that yield a sum of 7 are $1 + 6$, $2 + 5$, $3 + 4$, $4 + 3$, $5 + 2$, and $6 + 1$: 6 different combinations. Therefore, the probability of rolling a 7 is $\dfrac{6}{36}$, or $\dfrac{1}{6}$. To find the probability that this will happen twice in a row, you need to multiply: $\dfrac{1}{6} \times \dfrac{1}{6} = \dfrac{1}{36}$.

3. **85%:** There are two possible chains of events in which Bob will have the picnic:

One: The sun shines: $P = 70\%$ OR

Two: It rains AND Bob chooses to have the picnic anyway: $P = 30\%\left(\dfrac{1}{2}\right) = 15\%$

Add the probabilities together to find the total probability that Bob will have the picnic:

$70\% + 15\% = 85\%$

4. $\dfrac{16}{125}$: In order for Janet to receive a perfect score, neither of the previous two divers can receive one. Therefore, you are finding the probability of a chain of three events: that diver one will *not* get a perfect score AND diver two will *not* get a perfect score AND Janet *will* get a perfect score. Multiply the probabilities: $\dfrac{4}{5} \times \dfrac{4}{5} \times \dfrac{1}{5} = \dfrac{16}{125}$.

The probability is $\dfrac{16}{125}$ that Janet will receive a perfect score.

5. **40%:** Use an anagram model to find out the total number of different pairs the magician can pull out of his hat. Since two animals will be in the pair and the other three will not, use the "word" YYNNN.

A	B	C	D	E
Y	Y	N	N	N

$\dfrac{5!}{2!3!} = \dfrac{5 \times 4}{2 \times 1} = 10$

Thus, there are 10 possible pairs.

Then, list the pairs in which the animals will match. Represent the rabbits with the letters *a* and *b*, and the doves with the letters *x*, *y*, and *z*.

Matched Pairs: $R_a R_b$ $D_x D_y$ There are four pairs in which the animals
                      $D_x D_z$ $D_y D_z$ will be a matched set.

Therefore, the probability that the magician will randomly draw a matched set is $\dfrac{4}{10} = 40\%$.

Chapter 6

of

Number Properties

Extra Divisibility & Primes

In This Chapter...

Chapter 6

Extra Divisibility & Primes

This chapter covers harder material within the topic of divisibility and primes. Before you read this chapter, read the first four chapters of this book and complete some *Official Guide for GMAT Review* problems that involve divisibility and primes. If your goal is not 80th percentile (or higher) on the Quant section of the GMAT, you may want to skip this section.

Primes

You should become very comfortable with small prime numbers—at least the first 10. Even better, know (or be able to derive quickly) all the primes up to 100: 2, 3, 5, 7, 11, 13, 17, 19, 23, 29, 31, 37, 41, 43, 47, 53, 59, 61, 67, 71, 73, 79, 83, 89, 97. Here are some additional facts about primes that may be helpful on the GMAT:

- **There are an infinite number of prime numbers.** There is no upper limit to the size of prime numbers.

- **There is no simple pattern in the prime numbers.** Since 2 is the only even prime number, all other primes are odd. However, there is no easy pattern to determine which odd numbers will be prime. Each number needs to be tested directly to determine whether it is prime.

- **Positive integers with exactly two factors must be prime, and positive integers with more than two factors are never prime.** Any integer greater than or equal to 2 has at least two factors: 1 and itself. Thus, if there are only two factors of x (with x equal to an integer ≥ 2), then the factors of x *must* be 1 and x. Therefore, x must be prime. Also, do not forget that the number 1 is *not* prime. The number 1 has only one factor (itself), so it is defined as a non-prime number.

These facts can be used to disguise the topic of prime numbers on the GMAT. Take a look at the following Data Sufficiency (DS) examples:

> What is the value of integer x?
>
> (1) x has exactly 2 factors.
> (2) When x is divided by 2, the remainder is 0.

Statement (1) indicates that x is prime, because it has only 2 factors. This statement is insufficient by itself, since there are infinitely many prime numbers. Statement (2) indicates that 2 divides evenly into x, meaning that x is even; that is also insufficient by itself. Taken together, however, the two statements reveal that x must be an even prime—and the only even prime number is 2. The answer is (C).

> If x is a prime number, what is the value of x?
>
> (1) There are a total of 50 prime numbers between 2 and x, inclusive.
> (2) There is no integer n such that x is divisible by n and $1 < n < x$.

At first, this problem seems outlandishly difficult. How are you to list out the first 50 prime numbers in under two minutes? Remember, however, that this is a Data Sufficiency problem. You do not need to list the first 50 primes. Instead, all you need to do is determine *whether* you can do so.

For statement (1), you know that certain numbers are prime and others are not. You also know that x is prime. Therefore, if you were to list all the primes from 2 on up, you eventually would find the 50th prime number. That number must equal x: because x is prime, it *must* be the 50th item on that list of primes. This inforzvmation is sufficient.

For statement (2), you are told that x is not divisible by any integer greater than 1 and less than x. There fore, x can only have 1 and x as factors. In other words, x is prime. You already know this result, in fact: it was given to you in the question stem. So statement (2) does not help you determine what x is. This statement is insufficient.

The correct answer is **(A)**. (Incidentally, for those who are curious, the 50th prime number is 229.)

Divisibility and Addition/Subtraction

Part 1 of Divisibility & Primes showed that if you add or subtract multiples of an integer, you get another multiple of that integer. This rule can be generalized to other situations. For the two following rules, assume that N is an integer:

---

1. If you add a multiple of N to a non-multiple of N, the result is a non-multiple of N.
   (The same holds true for subtraction.) For example:
   $18 - 10 = 8$ (Multiple of 3) − (Non-multiple of 3) = (Non-multiple of 3)

MANHATTAN
PREP

2. If you add two non-multiples of N, the result could be either a multiple of N or a non-multiple of N. For example:

$19 + 13 = 32$ (Non-multiple of 3) + (Non-multiple of 3) = (Non-multiple of 3)

$19 + 14 = 33$ (Non-multiple of 3) + (Non-multiple of 3) = (Multiple of 3)

The exception to this rule is when $N = 2$. Two odds always sum to an even.

Try the following Data Sufficiency example:

Is N divisible by 7?

(1) $N = x - y$, where x and y are integers.
(2) x is divisible by 7, and y is not divisible by 7.

Statement (1) indicates that N is the difference between two integers (x and y), but it does not tell you anything about whether x or y is divisible by 7. This statement is insufficient.

Statement (2) tells you nothing about N. This statement is insufficient.

Statements (1) and (2) combined indicate that x is a multiple of 7, but y is not a multiple of 7. The difference between x and y can *never* be divisible by 7 if x is divisible by 7 but y is not. (If you are not convinced, try testing out some real numbers.) Therefore, N cannot be a multiple of 7.

The correct answer is (**C**).

Greatest Common Factor and Least Common Multiple

On the GMAT, you may have to find the greatest common factor (GCF) or least common multiple (LCM) of a set of two or more numbers.

> **The greatest common *factor* (GCF)** is the largest divisor of two or more integers; this *factor* will be smaller than or equal to the starting integers.

> **The least common *multiple* (LCM)** is the the smallest multiple of two or more integers; this *multiple* will be larger than or equal to the starting integers.

You may already know how to find the LCM. When you add together the fractions $\frac{1}{2} + \frac{1}{3} + \frac{1}{5}$, you convert the fractions to thirtieths: $\frac{1}{2} + \frac{1}{3} + \frac{1}{5} = \frac{15}{30} + \frac{10}{30} + \frac{6}{30} = \frac{31}{30}$. Why thirtieths? Because 30 is the LCM of the denominators 2, 3, and 5.

Finding GCF and LCM Using Venn Diagrams

You can find the GCF and LCM of two numbers by placing prime factors into a **Venn diagram**—a diagram of circles showing the overlapping and non-overlapping elements of two sets. To find the GCF and LCM of two numbers using a Venn diagram, perform the following steps:

1. Factor the numbers into primes. For example, $30 = 2 \times 3 \times 5$ and $24 = 2 \times 2 \times 2 \times 3$.

2. Create a Venn diagram.

3. Place each shared factor into the shared area of the diagram (the shaded region to the right). In this example, 30 and 24 share one 2 and one 3.

4. Place the remaining (non-shared) factors into the non-shared areas.

5. The GCF is the product of the primes in the shared region: $2 \times 3 = 6$.

6. The LCM is the product of all primes in the diagram: $5 \times 2 \times 3 \times 2 \times 2 = 120$.

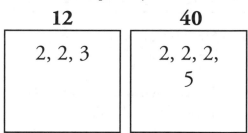

Try it an example:

Compute the GCF and LCM of 12 and 40 using the Venn diagram approach.

The prime factorizations of 12 and 40 are $2 \times 2 \times 3$ and $2 \times 2 \times 2 \times 5$, respectively:

The only common factors of 12 and 40 are two 2's. Therefore, place two 2's in the shared area of the Venn diagram and remove them from *both* prime factorizations. Then, place the remaining factors in the zones belonging exclusively to 12 and 40. These two outer regions must have *no* primes in common!

12	40
2, 2, 3	2, 2, 2, 5

The GCF of 12 and 40 is therefore $2 \times 2 = 4$, the product of the primes in the *shared area*. (An easy way to remember this is that the common factors are in the common area.)

The LCM is $3 \times 2 \times 2 \times 2 \times 5 = 120$, the product of *all* the primes in the diagram.

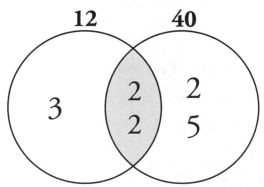

Note that if two numbers have *no* primes in common, then their GCF is 1 and their LCM is their product. For example, 35 ($= 5 \times 7$) and 6 ($= 2 \times 3$) have no prime numbers in common. Therefore, their GCF is 1 (the common factor of *all* positive integers) and their LCM is $35 \times 6 = 210$. Be careful: even though you have no primes in the common area, the GCF is not 0 but 1.

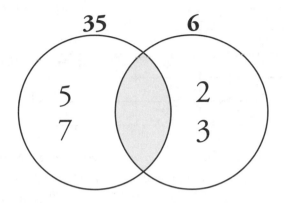

Advanced GCF and LCM Techniques

While Venn diagrams are helpful for visualizing the steps needed to compute the GCF and LCM, they can be cumbersome if you want to find the GCF or LCM of large numbers or of three or more numbers.

Finding GCF and LCM Using Prime Columns

Here are the steps:

    Step 1: Calculate the prime factors of each integer.

    Step 2: Create a column for each prime factor found within any of the integers.

    Step 3: Create a row for each integer.

    Step 4: In each cell of the table, place the prime factor raised to a *power*. This power counts how many copies of the column's prime factor appear in the prime box of the row's integer.

To calculate the GCF, take the *lowest* count of each prime factor found across *all* the integers. This counts the shared primes. To calculate the LCM, take the *highest* count of each prime factor found across *all* the integers. This counts all the primes less the shared primes.

Try this problem:

    Find the GCF and LCM of 100, 140, and 250.

    Step 1: Calculate the prime factors of each integer.

        $100 = 2 \times 2 \times 5 \times 5 = 2^2 \times 5^2$

        $140 = 2 \times 2 \times 5 \times 7 = 2^2 \times 5 \times 7$

        $250 = 2 \times 5 \times 5 \times 5 = 2 \times 5^3$

Step 2: Create a column for each prime factor base and a row for each integer. The different prime factors are 2, 5, and 7, so you need three columns. There are three integers (100, 140, and 250), so you also need three rows.

Step 3: Fill in the table with each prime factor raised to the appropriate power:

Number	2		5		7
100	2^2	×	5^2	×	7^0
140	2^2	×	5^1	×	7^1
250	2^1	×	5^3	×	7^0

To calculate the GCF, take the *smallest* count (the lowest power) in any column, because the GCF is formed only out of the *shared* primes. The smallest count of the factor 2 is one, in 250 (= $2^1 \times 5^3$). The smallest count of the factor 5 is one, in 140 (= $2^2 \times 5^1 \times 7^1$). The smallest count of the factor 7 is zero, since 7 does not appear in 100 or in 250. Therefore, the GCF is $2^1 \times 5^1 = 10$.

To calculate the LCM, take the *largest* count (the highest power) in any column, because the LCM is formed out of *all* the primes less the shared primes. The largest count of the factor 2 is two, in 140 and 100. The largest count of the factor 5 is three, in 250. The largest count of the factor 7 is one, in 140. Therefore, the LCM is $2^2 \times 5^3 \times 7^1 = 3,500$.

Number	2		5		7		
100	2^2	×	5^2	×	7^0		
140	2^2	×	5^1	×	7^1		
250	2^1	×	5^3	×	7^0		
GCF	2^1	×	5^1	×	7^0	=	$2^1 \times 5^1 = 10$
LCM	2^2	×	5^3	×	7^1	=	$2^2 \times 5^3 \times 7^1 = 3,500$

Finding GCF and LCM Using Prime Boxes or Factorizations

Also, you can use a shortcut directly from the prime boxes or the prime factorizations to find the GCF and LCM. Once you become familiar with the prime columns method, you can just scan the boxes or the factorizations and take all the lowest powers to find the GCF and the highest powers to find the LCM.

Try an example:

What are the GCF and LCM of 30 and 24?

30

2, 3, 5

24

2, 2, 2, 3

The prime factorization of 30 is $2 \times 3 \times 5$.
The prime factorization of 24 is $2 \times 2 \times 2 \times 3$, or $2^3 \times 3$.
The GCF is $2 \times 3 = 6$.
The LCM is $2^3 \times 3 \times 5 = 120$.

Finally, you may be asked to determine what combinations of numbers could lead to a specific GCF or LCM. This is a difficult task. Consider the following DS problem :

> Is the integer z divisible by 6?
>
> (1) The greatest common factor of z and 12 is 3.
> (2) The greatest common factor of z and 15 is 15.

When calculating the GCF for a set of numbers, determine the prime factors of each number and then take each prime factor to the *lowest* power it appears in any factorization. In this problem, you are given the GCF, so you can work backwards to determine what additional information can be determined.

Statement (1) indicates that z and 12 ($2 \times 2 \times 3$) have a GCF of 3. Set up that information in a prime columns table (like the one on the right) to figure out what you can deduce about the prime factors of z.

Notice that the GCF of 12 and z contains a 3. Since the GCF contains each prime factor to the power it appears the *least*, you know that z must also contain at least one 3. Therefore, z is divisible by 3.

Number	2	3
z	–	3^1
12	2^2	3^1

Notice also that the GCF contains NO 2's. Since 12 contains two 2's, z must not contain any 2's. Therefore, z is *not* divisible by 2. Since z is not divisible by 2, it cannot be divisible by 6. This statement is sufficient.

Statement (2) indicates that z and 15 (3×5) have a GCF of 15. Set that up in a prime columns table (see below) to figure out what you can deduce about the prime factors of z.

The GCF of 15 and z contains a 3. Since the GCF contains each prime factor to the power it appears the *least*, you know that z must also contain at least one 3. Therefore, z is divisible by 3.

Number	3	5
z	3^1	5^1
15	3^1	5^1

Likewise, z must also contain a 5. Therefore, z is divisible by 5.

However, this does *not* indicate whether z contains any 2's. In order to be divisible by 6, z has to contain at least one 2 and at least one 3. Thus, it's impossible to tell whether z is divisible by 6; this statement is not sufficient. The correct answer is **(A)**.

Now consider this example:

> If the LCM of a and 12 is 36, what are the possible values of a?

As in the earlier example, you can use the prime columns technique to draw conclusions about the prime factors of a.

First, notice that *a* cannot be larger than 36. The LCM of two or more integers is always *at least* as large as any of the integers. Therefore, the maximum value of *a* is 36.

Next, the prime factorization of 36 is $2 \times 2 \times 3 \times 3$. Notice that the LCM of 12 and *a* contains two 2's. Since the LCM contains each prime factor to the power it appears the *most*, and since 12 also contains two 2's, *a* cannot contain more than two 2's. It does not necessarily need to contain any 2's, so *a* can contain zero, one, or two 2's.

Finally, observe that the LCM of 12 and *a* contains two 3's. But 12 only contains *one* 3. The 3^2 factor in the LCM must have come from the prime factorization of *a*. Therefore, *a* contains exactly two 3's.

Number	2	3
a	$\leq 2^2$	3^2
12	2^2	3^1

Since *a* must contain exactly two 3's, and can contain no 2's, one 2, or two 2's, *a* could be $3 \times 3 = 9$, $3 \times 3 \times 2 = 18$, or $3 \times 3 \times 2 \times 2 = 36$. Thus, 9, 18, and 36 are the possible values of *a*.

Other Applications of Primes & Divisibility

Counting Factors and Primes

The GMAT can ask you to count factors of some number in several different ways. For example, consider the number 1,400. The prime factorization of this number is $2 \times 2 \times 2 \times 5 \times 5 \times 7$, or $2^3 \times 5^2 \times 7$. Here are three different questions that the GMAT could ask you about this integer:

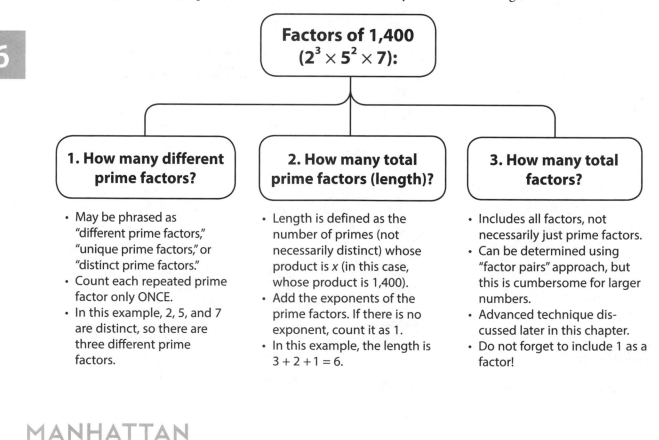

Factors of 1,400 ($2^3 \times 5^2 \times 7$):

1. How many different prime factors?

- May be phrased as "different prime factors," "unique prime factors," or "distinct prime factors."
- Count each repeated prime factor only ONCE.
- In this example, 2, 5, and 7 are distinct, so there are three different prime factors.

2. How many total prime factors (length)?

- Length is defined as the number of primes (not necessarily distinct) whose product is *x* (in this case, whose product is 1,400).
- Add the exponents of the prime factors. If there is no exponent, count it as 1.
- In this example, the length is $3 + 2 + 1 = 6$.

3. How many total factors?

- Includes all factors, not necessarily just prime factors.
- Can be determined using "factor pairs" approach, but this is cumbersome for larger numbers.
- Advanced technique discussed later in this chapter.
- Do not forget to include 1 as a factor!

Consider the number 252.
  (a)   How many unique prime factors of 252 are there?
  (b)   What is the length of 252 (as defined above)?
  (c)   How many total factors of 252 are there?

For (a), determine the number of unique prime factors by looking at the prime factorization of 252: $2 \times 2 \times 3 \times 3 \times 7$. There are three different prime factors in 252: 2, 3, and 7. Do *not* count repeated primes to answer this particular question.

For (b), the "length" of an integer is defined as the total number of primes that, when multiplied together, equal that integer. (Note: on the GMAT, any question that asks about the length of an integer will provide this definition of length, so you do not need to memorize it.) The prime factorization of 252 is $2 \times 2 \times 3 \times 3 \times 7$. There are five total prime factors in 252: 2, 2, 3, 3, and 7. In other words, the length of an integer is just the total number of primes in the prime box of that integer. *Do* count repeated primes to answer this particular question.

You can also answer this question by looking at the prime factorization in exponential form: $252 = 2^2 \times 3^2 \times 7$. Add the exponents: $2 + 2 + 1 = 5$. Notice that a number written in this form without an exponent has an implicit exponent of 1.

For (c), one way to determine the total number of factors is to determine the factor pairs of 252, using the process described in Chapter 1 of this book and shown in the chart to the right. Simply start at 1 and "walk up" through all the integers, determining whether each is a factor, as shown in the table. You can stop once the small column "meets" the large column. For example, since the last entry in the large column is 18, you can stop searching once you have evaluated 17 as a possible factor. Count up the number of factors in the table: there are 18.

Small	Large
1	252
2	126
3	84
4	63
6	42
7	36
9	28
12	21
14	18

This method will be too cumbersome for larger numbers, so a more advanced method is introduced in the next section.

Counting Total Factors

When a problem has a large number of factors, the factor pair method can be too slow. Therefore, you need a general method to apply to more difficult problems of this type. For example:

How many different factors does 2,000 have?

It would take a very long time to list all of the factors of 2,000. However, prime factorization can shorten the process considerably. First, factor 2,000 into primes: $2,000 = 2^4 \times 5^3$. The key to this method is to consider each distinct prime factor separately.

Consider the prime factor 2 first. Because the prime factorization of 2,000 contains four 2's, there are *five* possibilities for the number of 2's in any factor of 2,000: none, one, two, three, or four. (Do not forget the possibility of *no* occurrences! For example, 5 is a factor of 2,000, and 5 does not have *any* 2's in its prime box.)

Next, consider the prime factor 5. There are three 5's, so there are *four* possibilities for the number of 5's in a factor of 2,000: none, one, two, or three. (Again, do not forget the possibility of *no* occurrences of 5.)

In general, if a prime factor appears to the Nth power, then there are $(N + 1)$ possibilities for the occurrences of that prime factor. This is true for each of the individual prime factors of any number.

You can borrow a principle from combinatorics to simplify the calculation of the number of prime factors in 2,000: when you are making a number of separate decisions, then multiply the number of ways to make each *individual* decision to find the number of ways to make *all* the decisions. Because there are five possible decisions for the 2 factor and four possible decisions for the 5 factor, there are $5 \times 4 = 20$ different factors.

The logic behind this process can also be represented in the following table of factors. (Note that there is no reason to make this table, unless you are interested in the specific factors themselves. It simply illustrates the reasoning behind multiplying the possibilities.)

	2^0	2^1	2^2	2^3	2^4
5^0	1	2	4	8	16
5^1	5	10	20	40	80
5^2	25	50	100	200	400
5^3	125	250	500	1,000	2,000

Each entry in the table is the unique product of a power of 2 (the columns) and a power of 5 (the rows). For instance, $50 = 2^1 \times 5^2$. Notice that the factor in the top left corner contains no 5's and no 2's. That factor is 1 (which equals $2^0 \times 5^0$).

The table has five columns (representing the possible powers of 2 in the factor) and four rows (representing the possible powers of 5 in the factor). The total number of factors is given by 5 columns multiplied by 4 rows, so there are 20 different factors.

Although a table like the one above cannot be easily set up for more than two prime factors, the process can be generalized to numbers with more than two prime factors. If a number has prime factorization $a^x \times b^y \times c^z$ (where a, b, and c are all prime), then the number has $(x + 1)(y + 1)(z + 1)$ different factors.

For instance, $9,450 = 2^1 \times 3^3 \times 5^2 \times 7^1$, so 9,450 has $(1 + 1)(3 + 1)(2 + 1)(1 + 1) = 48$ different factors.

Perfect Squares, Cubes, etc.

The GMAT occasionally tests properties of perfect squares, which are squares of other integers. The numbers 4 (= 2^2) and 25 (= 5^2) are examples of perfect squares. One special property of perfect squares is that **all perfect squares have an odd number of total factors**. Similarly, any integer that has an odd number of total factors *must* be a perfect square. All other non-square integers have an even number of factors. Why is this the case?

Think back to the factor pair exercises you have done so far. Factors come in pairs. If a and b are integers and $a \times b = c$, then a and b are a factor pair of c. However, if c is a perfect square, then in *one* of its factor pairs, a equals b. That is, in this particular pair you have $a \times a = c$, or $a^2 = c$. This "pair" does not consist of two different factors. Rather, you have a single unpaired factor: the square root.

Consider the perfect square 36. It has 5 factor pairs that yield 36, as shown to the right. Notice that the *final* pair is 6 and 6, so instead of $5 \times 2 = 10$ total factors, there are only 9 different factors of 36.

Small	Large
1	36
2	18
3	12
4	9
6	6

Notice also that any number that is not a perfect square will *never* have an odd number of factors. That is because the only way to arrive at an odd number of factors is to have a factor pair in which the two factors are equal.

For larger numbers, it would be much more difficult to use the factor pair technique to prove that a number is a perfect square or that it has an odd number of factors. Thankfully, you can use a different approach. Notice that perfect squares are formed from the product of two copies of the same prime factors. For instance, $90^2 = (2 \times 3^2 \times 5)(2 \times 3^2 \times 5) = 2^2 \times 3^4 \times 5^2$. Therefore, **the prime factorization of a perfect square contains only even powers of primes**. It is also true that any number whose prime factorization contains only even powers of primes must be a perfect square.

Here are some examples:

$$144 = 2^4 \times 3^2 \qquad\qquad 9 = 3^2$$
$$36 = 2^2 \times 3^2 \qquad\qquad 40,000 = 2^6 \times 5^4$$

All of these integers are perfect squares.

By contrast, if a number's prime factorization contains any odd powers of primes, then the number is not a perfect square. For instance, $132,300 = 2^2 \times 3^3 \times 5^2 \times 7^2$ is not a perfect square, because the 3 is raised to an odd power.

The same logic used for perfect squares extends to perfect cubes and to other "perfect" powers. If a number is a perfect cube, then it is formed from three identical sets of primes, so all the powers of primes are multiples of 3 in the factorization of a perfect cube: for instance: $90^3 = (2 \times 3^2 \times 5)(2 \times 3^2 \times 5)(2 \times 3^2 \times 5) = 2^3 \times 3^6 \times 5^3$.

6

Try an example:

If k^3 is divisible by 240, what is the least possible value of integer k?

   (A) 12   (B) 30   (C) 60   (D) 90   (E) 120

The prime box of k^3 contains the prime factors of 240, which are 2, 2, 2, 2, 3, and 5. The prime factors of k^3 should be the prime factors of k appearing in sets of three, so distribute the prime factors of k^3 into three columns to represent the prime factors of k, as shown to the right.

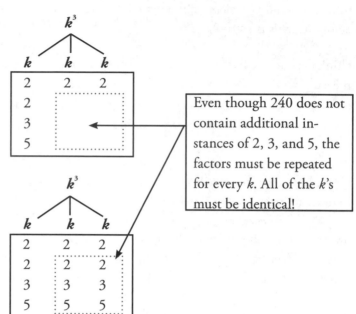

Even though 240 does not contain additional instances of 2, 3, and 5, the factors must be repeated for every k. All of the k's must be identical!

There is a complete set of three 2's in the prime box of k^3, so k must have a factor of 2. However, there is a fourth 2 left over. That additional factor of 2 must be from k as well, so assign it to one of the component k columns. There is an incomplete set of 3's in the prime box of k^3, but you can still infer that k has a factor of 3; otherwise k^3 would not have any. Similarly, k^3 has a single 5 in its prime box, but that factor must be one of the factors of k as well. Thus, k has 2, 2, 3, and 5 in its prime box, so k must be a multiple of 60.

The correct answer is **(C)**.

Factorials and Divisibility

Because $N!$ is the product of all the integers from 1 to N, $N!$ must be divisible by all integers from 1 to N. Another way of saying this is that $N!$ is a multiple of all the integers from 1 to N.

This fact works in concert with other properties of divisibility and multiples. For instance, the quantity $10! + 7$ must be a multiple of 7, because both $10!$ and 7 are multiples of 7.

Therefore, $10! + 15$ must be a multiple of 15, because $10!$ is divisible by 5 and 3, and 15 is divisible by 5 and 3. Thus, both numbers are divisible by 15, and the sum is divisible by 15. Finally, $10! + 11!$ is a multiple of any integer from 1 to 10, because every integer between 1 and 10 inclusive is a factor of both $10!$ and $11!$, separately.

6

Advanced Remainders

Remainders are often expressed as integers; however, they can also be expressed as fractions or as decimals. It is important to understand the connection between these three different ways of expressing remainders.

How can you express 17 divided by 5 using remainders? It can be expressed as $17 = 3 \times 5 + 2$. Divide both sides of the equation by 5 (because the initial problem was to divide 17 by 5):

$$\frac{17}{5} = 3 + \frac{2}{5}$$

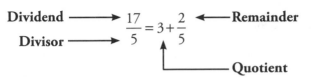

The fraction form of a remainder is the integer form divided by the divisor. And, as you may have guessed, the decimal form of a remainder is just the decimal equivalent of the fraction: $\frac{2}{5} = 0.4$.

The quotient can be 0. For instance, when 3 is divided by 5, the solution is 0 remainder 3, because 5 goes into 3 zero times with 3 left over.

In sum, you can express the division of 17 by 5 in three ways:

$$\frac{17}{5} = 3 \text{ with a remainder of } 2 \qquad \frac{17}{5} = 3\frac{2}{5} \qquad \frac{17}{5} = 3.4$$

Try the following example:

> When positive integer A is divided by positive integer B, the result is 4.35. Which of the following could be the remainder when A is divided by B?
>
> (A) 13   (B) 14   (C) 15   (D) 16   (E) 17

It may seem as if this question has not given you a whole lot to go on. First, notice the language in the question. When a GMAT question refers to a remainder, it is referring to the integer form of the remainder. The key to this problem will be to connect the integer form of the remainder with the decimal form of the remainder provided in the question.

You know that $\frac{A}{B} = 4.35$. That means that 4 is the quotient and 0.35 is the remainder (expressed as a decimal). If you let R equal the remainder, then you can set up the following relationship:

$$0.35 = \frac{\text{Remainder}}{\text{Divisor}} = \frac{R}{B}$$

This relationship may not appear particularly useful. The value, however, comes from a hidden constraint of this relationship: R and B must both be integers. You know B is an integer because of information given in the question. And you know that R is an integer because this relationship is the connection between the integer form of remainders and the decimal (or fraction) form.

The next step is to change the decimal to a fraction:

$$0.35 = \frac{R}{B}$$
$$\frac{35}{100} = \frac{R}{B}$$
$$\frac{7}{20} = \frac{R}{B}$$

Now the decimal remainder is expressed as a division involving two integers (7 and 20).

Finally, cross multiply the fractions:

$$7B = 20R$$

In order for this equation to involve only integers, the prime factors on the left side of the equation must equal the prime factors on the right side of the equation. You know that the divisor (B) *must* be a multiple of 20 and, more importantly, the remainder (R) *must* be a multiple of 7.

Take a look at the answer choices. The only choice that is a multiple of 7 is answer (B) 14. Therefore, the correct answer is **(B)**.

You could even use this information to calculate the values of A and B.

First, go back to the original relationship you wrote down:

$$0.35 = \frac{\text{Remainder}}{\text{Divisor}} = \frac{R}{B}$$

You now know a possible remainder, so replace R with (14):

$$0.35 = \frac{R}{B}$$
$$\frac{7}{20} = \frac{14}{B}$$
$$\left(\frac{7}{20}\right)B = 14$$
$$B = 14 \times \frac{20}{7} = 2 \times 20 = 40$$

You can then use the value of B to solve for A:

$$\frac{A}{B} = 4.35$$
$$\frac{A}{(40)} = 4.35$$
$$A = 4.35 \times 40 = 174$$

MANHATTAN
PREP

Creating Numbers with a Certain Remainder

Occasionally, a GMAT question will give you the following type of information:

"When positive integer n is divided by 7, there is a remainder of 2."

To answer this question, you will need to be able to list different possible values of n.

So, what are the possible values of n? Since the remainder is given to you as an integer, set up the integer remainder relationship:

Dividend = Quotient × Divisor + Remainder

n = (integer) ×   7   +   2

Perform two calculations to generate possible values of n: first, multiply 7 by an integer and, second, add 2 to that product, as in the chart below:

Integer (Quotient)	×	7 (Divisor)	+	2 (Remainder)	=	n (Dividend)
0	×	7	+	2	=	2
1	×	7	+	2	=	9
2	×	7	+	2	=	16
3	×	7	+	2	=	23

Another way to think of all these values of n is that they are 2 more than a multiple of 7. Remember that 0 is a multiple of *any* number. In this example, 2 divided by 7 has a quotient of 0 and a remainder of 2.

Notice also that the possible values of n follow a pattern: the successive value of n is 7 more than the previous value. You can keep adding 7 to generate more possible values for n.

On the GMAT, it will be fairly straightforward to calculate possible values of n. Focus on the *important* or relevant values. Try the following example:

> When positive integer x is divided by 5, the remainder is 2. When positive integer y is divided by 4, the remainder is 1. Which of the following values CANNOT be the sum of x and y?
>
> (A) 12   (B) 13   (C) 14   (D) 16   (E) 21

To answer this question efficiently, you will need to list out possible values of x and y. Notice that the answer choices are not very large. Listing out a few of the smallest possibilities for x and y should be sufficient:

$x = 2, 7, 12, 17$
$y = 1, 5, 9, 13$

6

The answer choices represent potential values for $x + y$. Which answers can you create from your list of possible values for x and y?

(A) $12 = 7 + 5$

(B) $13 = 12 + 1$

(C) $14 = $???

(D) $16 = 7 + 9$

(E) $21 = 12 + 9$

The correct answer is **(C)**. There is no way for $x + y$ to equal 14.

Problem Set

1. If $y = 30p$, and p is prime, what is the greatest common factor of y and $14p$, in terms of p?

2. What is the greatest common factor of 420 and 660?

3. What is the least common multiple of 18 and 24?

4. Is p divisible by 168?

   (1) p is divisible by 14.
   (2) p is divisible by 12.

5. Is pq divisible by 168?

   (1) p is divisible by 14.
   (2) q is divisible by 12.

6. What is the greatest common factor of x and y?

   (1) x and y are both divisible by 4.
   (2) $x - y = 4$

7. What is the value of integer x?

   (1) The least common multiple of x and 45 is 225.
   (2) The least common multiple of x and 20 is 300.

8. If x^2 is divisible by 216, what is the smallest possible value for positive integer x?

9. If x and y are positive integers and $x \div y$ has a remainder of 5, what is the smallest possible value of xy?

10. All of the following have the same set of unique prime factors EXCEPT:

    (A) 420   (B) 490   (C) 560   (D) 700   (E) 980

11. Which of the following numbers is NOT prime? (Hint: avoid actually computing these numbers.)

    (A) $6! - 1$ (B) $6! + 21$ (C) $6! + 41$ (D) $7! - 1$ (E) $7! + 11$

6

Solutions

1. **2p:** The greatest common factor of y (= $30p$) and $14p$ is the product of all the common prime factors, using the lower power of repeated factors. The only repeated factors are 2 and p: $2^1 \times p^1 = 2 \times p = 2p$. Again, you would get the same answer if p were any positive integer.

Number	2		3		5		7		p
$30p$	2^1	×	3^1	×	5^1	–		×	p^1
$14p$	2^1	–		–		×	7^1	×	p^1
GCF	2^1								p^1

2. **60:**

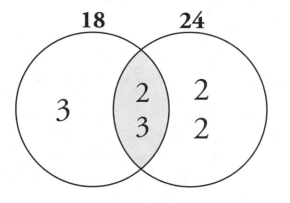

$420 = 2 \times 2 \times 3 \times 5 \times 7$
$660 = 2 \times 2 \times 3 \times 5 \times 11$
The greatest common factor is the product of the primes in the shared factors *only*: $2 \times 2 \times 3 \times 5 = 60$.

3. **72:**

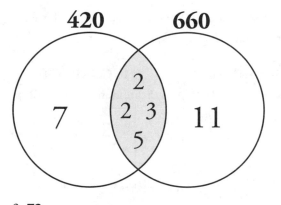

$18 = 2 \times 3 \times 3$
$24 = 2 \times 2 \times 2 \times 3$
The least common multiple is the product of all the primes in the diagram: $3 \times 2 \times 3 \times 2 \times 2 = 72$.

4. **(E):** The first step in this kind of problem is to determine what prime factors p needs in order to be divisible by 168. The prime factorization of 168 is $2 \times 2 \times 2 \times 3 \times 7$, so the question can be restated as follows:

Are there at least three 2's, one 3, and one 7 in the prime box of p?

(1) INSUFFICIENT: Statement (1) tells you that p is divisible by 14, which is 2×7. Therefore, you know that p has at least a 2 and a 7 in its prime box. However, you do not know anything else about the possible prime factors in p, so you cannot determine whether p is divisible by 168. For example, p could equal $2 \times 2 \times 2 \times 3 \times 7 = 168$, in which case the answer to the question would be, "Yes, p is di-

168

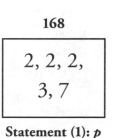

2, 2, 2,
3, 7

Statement (1): p

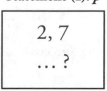

2, 7
… ?

visible by 168." Alternatively, p could equal $2 \times 7 = 14$, in which case the answer to the question would be, "No, p is *not* divisible by 168."

(2) INSUFFICIENT: Statement (2) tells you that p is divisible by 12, which is $2 \times 2 \times 3$. Therefore, you know that p has at least two 2's and one 3 in its prime box. However, you do not know anything else about p, so you cannot determine whether p is divisible by 168. For example, p could equal 168, in which case the answer to the question would be, "Yes, p is divisible by 168." Alternatively, p could equal 12, in which case the answer to the question would be "No, p is *not* divisible by 168."

Statement (2): p

2, 2, 3
… ?

(1) AND (2) INSUFFICIENT: Combining the primes from statements (1) and (2), you seem to have three 2's, one 3, and one 7. That should be sufficient to prove that p is divisible by 168.

However, you cannot do this. Consider the number 84: 84 is divisible by 14 and it is also divisible by 12. Therefore, following from statements (1) and (2), p could be 84. However, 84 is not divisible by 168: $84 = 2 \times 2 \times 3 \times 7$, so you are missing a needed 2.

INCORRECT:
Statement's (1) & (2): p

2, 2, 2
3, 7, … ?

Both statements mention that p contains at least one 2 in its prime factorization. It is possible that these statements are referring to the *same* 2. Therefore, one of the 2's in statement (2) *overlaps* with the 2 from statement (1). You have been given *redundant* information. The two boxes you made for statements (1) and (2) are not truly different boxes. Rather, they are two different views of the same box (the prime box of p).

Thus, you have to eliminate the redundant 2 when you combine the two views of p's prime box from statements (1) and (2). Given both statements, you only know that p has two 2's, one 3, and one 7 in its prime box. The correct answer is (**E**).

5. (**C**): How is this problem different from problem 4? A new variable, q, has been introduced, and you're now told that q is divisible by 12 (rather than p). Because of this change, the information in the two statements is no longer redundant. There is no overlap between the prime boxes, because the prime boxes belong to different variables (p and q). Statement (1) tells you that p has at least one 2 and one 7 in its prime box. Statement (2) tells you that q has at least two 2's and one 3 in its prime box. As with question 4, the two statements individually are not sufficient to answer the question, so you can eliminate answers (A), (B), and (D). When you combine the two statements, you combine the prime boxes without removing any overlap, because there is no such overlap. As a result, you know that the product pq contains *at least* three 2's, one 3, and one 7 in its combined prime box. You can now answer the question "Is pq divisible by 168?" with a definitive "Yes," since the question is really asking whether pq contains *at least* three 2's, one 3, and one 7 in its prime box.

The correct answer to this problem is (**C**).

6. **(C):** (1) INSUFFICIENT: Statement (1) tells you that x and y are both divisible by 4, but that does not tell you the GCF of x and y. For example, if $x = 16$ and $y = 20$, then the GCF is 4. However, if $x = 16$ and $y = 32$, then the GCF is 16.

(2) INSUFFICIENT: Statement (2) tells you that $x - y = 4$, but that does not tell you the GCF of x and y. For example, if $x = 1$ and $y = 5$, then the GCF is 1. However, if $x = 16$ and $y = 20$, then the GCF is 4.

(1) AND (2) SUFFICIENT: Combined, statements (1) and (2) tell you that x and y are multiples of 4 and that they are 4 apart on the number line. Therefore, **x and y are consecutive multiples of 4**. Since x and y are consecutive multiples of 4, their GCF must equal 4 (test some consecutive multiples of 4 to see that this is true). The correct answer is **(C)**.

7. **(C):** Try to determine the value of x using the LCM of x and certain other integers.

(1) INSUFFICIENT: Statement (1) tells you that x and 45 ($3 \times 3 \times 5$) have an LCM of 225 ($= 3 \times 3 \times 5 \times 5 = 3^2 \times 5^2$).

Notice on the chart to the right that the LCM of x and 45 contains two 3's. Because 45 contains two 3's, x can contain zero, one, or two 3's. The LCM of x and 45 contains two 5's. Because 45 contains only ONE 5, x must contain **exactly** two 5's. (If x contained more 5's, the LCM would contain more 5's. If x contained fewer 5's, the LCM would contain fewer 5's.)

Number	3		5
x	?	×	?
45	3^2	×	5^1
LCM	3^2	×	5^2

Therefore, x can be any of the following numbers:

$$x = 5 \times 5 = 25$$
$$x = 3 \times 5 \times 5 = 75$$
$$x = 3 \times 3 \times 5 \times 5 = 225$$

(2) INSUFFICIENT: Statement (2) tells you that x and 20 ($2 \times 2 \times 5$) have an LCM of 300 ($= 2 \times 2 \times 3 \times 5 \times 5 = 2^2 \times 3^1 \times 5^2$).

The LCM of x and 20 contains two 2's. Because 20 contains two 2's, x can contain zero, one, or two 2's. The LCM of x and 20 contains one 3. Because 20 contains no 3's, x must contain **exactly** one 3.

Number	2		3		5
x	?	×	?	×	?
20	2^2		–	×	5^1
LCM	2^2	×	3^1	×	5^2

Furthermore, the LCM of x and 20 contains two 5's. Because 20 contains one 5, x must contain **exactly** two 5's.

Therefore, x can be any of the following numbers:

$$x = 3 \times 5 \times 5 = 75.$$
$$x = 2 \times 3 \times 5 \times 5 = 150.$$
$$x = 2 \times 2 \times 3 \times 5 \times 5 = 300.$$

(1) AND (2) SUFFICIENT: Statement (1) tells you that x could be 25, 75, or 225. Statement (2) tells you that x could be 75, 150, or 300. The only number that satisfies both of these conditions is $x = 75$. Therefore, you know that x must be 75. The correct answer is **(C)**.

8. 36: The prime box of x^2 contains the prime factors of 216, which are 2, 2, 2, 3, 3, and 3. You know that the prime factors of x^2 should be the prime factors of x appearing in sets of two, or pairs. Therefore, you should distribute the prime factors of x^2 into two columns to represent the prime factors of x, as shown to the right.

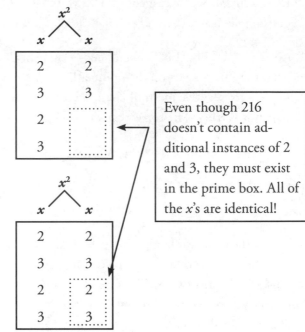

Even though 216 doesn't contain additional instances of 2 and 3, they must exist in the prime box. All of the x's are identical!

There is a complete pair of two 2's in the prime box of x^2, so x must have a factor of 2. However, there is a third 2 left over. That additional factor of 2 must be from x as well, so assign it to one of the component x columns. Also, there is a complete pair of two 3's in the prime box of x^2, so x must have a factor of 3. However, there is a third 3 left over. That additional factor of 3 must be from x as well, so assign it to one of the component x columns. Thus, x has 2, 3, 2, and 3 in its prime box, so x must be a positive multiple of 36.

9. 30: The remainder must always be smaller than the divisor. In this problem, 5 must be smaller than y. Additionally, y must be an integer, so y must be at least 6. If y is 6, then the smallest possible value of x is 5. (Other values of x that leave a remainder of 5 when divided by 6 would be 11, 17, 23, etc.) If y is chosen to be larger than 6, then the smallest possible value of x is still 5. Thus, you will get the smallest possible value of the product xy by choosing the smallest x together with the smallest y. The smallest possible value of xy is $5 \times 6 = 30$.

10. (A): To solve this problem, take the prime factorization of each answer choice and note the unique prime factors. One of the answer choices will have a different set of unique prime factors than the other answer choices:

(A) $420 = 42 \times 10 = 21 \times 2 \times 2 \times 5 = 3 \times 7 \times 2 \times 2 \times 5$. (Unique primes: 2, 3, 5, and 7)
(B) $490 = 49 \times 10 = 7 \times 7 \times 2 \times 5$ (Unique primes: 2, 5, and 7)
(C) $560 = 56 \times 10 = 7 \times 8 \times 2 \times 5 = 7 \times 2 \times 2 \times 2 \times 2 \times 5$. (Unique primes: 2, 5, and 7)
(D) $700 = 70 \times 10 = 7 \times 2 \times 5 \times 2 \times 5$ (Unique primes: 2, 5, and 7)
(E) $980 = 98 \times 10 = 49 \times 2 \times 2 \times 5 = 7 \times 7 \times 2 \times 2 \times 5$. (Unique primes: 2, 5, and 7)

The correct answer is **(A)**, because it is the only answer choice with a prime factor of 3.

11. **(B):** You could solve this problem by computing each answer choice and testing each one to see whether it is divisible by any smaller integer. However, some of the numbers in the answer choices will be very large (e.g., 7! is equal to 5,040), so testing to see whether these numbers are prime will be extremely time consuming.

A different approach can be taken: try to find an answer choice that *cannot* be prime based on the properties of divisibility. Earlier in this chapter, you learned the following property of factorials and divisibility: $N!$ is a multiple of all integers from 1 to N. In Chapter 1, you also learned that if two numbers share a factor, their sum or difference also shares the same factor. You can apply these concepts directly to the answer choices:

  (A) 6! − 1: 6! is not prime, but 6! − 1 might be prime, because 6! and 1 do not share any prime factors.

  (B) 6! + 21: 6! is not prime, and 6! + 21 CANNOT be prime, because 6! and 21 are both multiples of 3. Therefore, 6! + 21 is divisible by 3.

  (C) 6! + 41: 6! is not prime, but 6! + 41 might be prime, because 6! and 41 do not share any prime factors.

  (D) 7! − 1: 7! is not prime, but 7! − 1 might be prime, because 7! and 1 do not share any prime factors.

  (E) 7! + 11: 7! is not prime, but 7! + 11 might be prime, because 7! and 11 do not share any prime factors.

By the way, because answer (B) cannot be prime, you can infer that all the other answer choices *must* be prime, without having to actually check them. There *cannot* be more than one correct answer choice.

6

Chapter 7
of
Number Properties

Extra Combinatorics
& Probability

In This Chapter...

Chapter 7
Extra Combinatorics & Probability

Disguised Combinatorics

Some combinatorics problems are written disguise, with problem statements that seem to bear little resemblance to the typical examples shown earlier in the general combinatorics chapter. If you are not aiming for a 90th percentile or higher score on the GMAT, consider skipping this section.

Many word problems involving the words "how many" are combinatorics problems. Also, many combinatorics problems masquerade as probability problems. The difficult part of the problem draws on combinatorics to count desired or total possibilities, whereas creating the probability fraction is trivial. If you think creatively enough, looking for *analogies* to known problem types, you may be able to find a viable combinatorics solution.

Here are some examples of combinatorics problems that at first may appear to have little to do with combinatorics:

- How many four-digit integers have digits with some specified properties?
- How many paths exist from point A to point B in a given diagram?
- How many diagonals, triangles, lines, etc., exist in a given geometrical figure?
- How many *pairings* (handshakes, games between two teams, nonstop flights between cities, etc.) exist in a given situation? (Pairings are groups of two.)

Try this example:

> Alicia lives in a town whose streets are on a grid system, with all streets running east–west or north–south without breaks. Her school, located on a corner, lies three blocks south and three blocks east of her home, also located on a corner. If Alicia only walks south or east on her way to school, how many possible routes can she take to school?

First, draw a diagram of the situation:

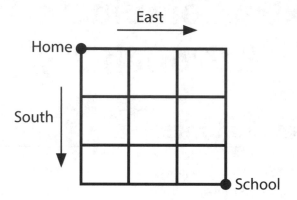

It may be tempting to draw all the different routes, but this method will be time consuming. Fortunately, you can answer this question using combinatorics.

Alicia will have to walk south 3 times and east 3 times on her way to school. That's 6 blocks in total that she'll walk. She'll have to make 6 decisions total: to walk south or east at each corner. For instance, she could walk south–east–east–south–south–east to get to her goal.

You're arranging 6 decisions. But you also have repeats: 3 blocks south and 3 blocks east. Divide 6! by 3! and 3!:

$$\frac{6!}{3!3!} = \frac{6 \times 5 \times 4 \times 3!}{3 \times 2 \times 1 \times 3!} = 5 \times 4 = 20$$

There are 20 routes to school.

You could also have made an anagram grid of the situation:

1	2	3	4	5	6
S	S	S	E	E	E

How many anagrams can you make of the "word" SSSEEE? You can make 6! divided by the product of 3! and 3!.

Arrangements with Constraints

The most complex combinatorics problems include unusual constraints: one person refuses to sit next to another, for example. Try the following:

> Greg, Marcia, Peter, Jan, Bobby, and Cindy go to a movie and sit next to each other in six adjacent seats in the front row of the theater. If Marcia and Jan will not sit next to each other, in how many different arrangements can the six people sit?

This is a simple arrangement with one unusual constraint: Marcia and Jan will not sit next to each other. To solve the problem, ignore the constraint for now. Just find the number of ways in which 6 people can sit in 6 chairs:

$$6! = 6 \times 5 \times 4 \times 3 \times 2 \times 1 = 720$$

Because of the constraint on Jan and Marcia, though, not all of those 720 seating arrangements are viable. Count the arrangements in which Jan *is* sitting next to Marcia (the *undesirable* seating arrangements), and subtract them from the total of 720.

To count the ways in which Jan *must* sit next to Marcia, use the **glue method**:

> For problems in which items or people must be next to each other, pretend that the items are glued together into one larger item.

Imagine that Jan and Marcia are stuck together into one person. There are now effectively 5 people: JM (stuck together), G, P, B, and C. These 5 people can be arranged in $5! = 120$ different ways.

Each of those 120 different ways, though, represents *two* different possibilities, because the "stuck together" moviegoers could be in order either as J–M or as M–J. Therefore, the total number of seating arrangements with Jan next to Marcia is $2 \times 120 = 240$.

Finally, do not forget that those 240 possibilities are the ones to be *excluded* from consideration. The number of allowed seating arrangements is therefore $720 - 240$, or 480.

7

The Domino Effect

Sometimes the outcome of the first event will affect the probability of a subsequent event. For example:

> A box contains 10 blocks, 3 of which are red. If you pick two blocks out of the box, what is the probability that they are both red? Assume that you do NOT replace the first block after you have picked it.

You're asked to find the probability of a red AND a red, so calculate the probability of each event and multiply the numbers together.

The probability of selecting a red block on the first try is $\dfrac{3}{10}$. But, for the second try, you now have only 9 blocks to choose from, and only 2 red blocks, so the probability of selecting a red block on the second try is $\dfrac{2}{9}$. Now multiply.

$$\frac{3}{10} \times \frac{2}{9} = \frac{\cancel{3}^{1}}{\cancel{10}^{5}} \times \frac{\cancel{2}^{1}}{\cancel{9}^{3}} = \frac{1}{15}$$

Thus, the probability of picking two reds is $\dfrac{1}{15}$.

Do not forget to consider whether one event affects subsequent events. The first roll of a die or flip of a coin has no effect on any subsequent rolls or flips. However, the first pick of an object out of a box does affect subsequent picks if you do not replace that object. Check whether the object is or is not placed back into the container before the second and subsequent picks.

Combinatorics and the Domino Effect

The **domino-effect rule** states that you multiply the probabilities of events in a sequence, taking earlier events into account. Some domino-effect problems are difficult because of the sheer number of possibilities involved. When all possibilities are equivalent, though, combinatorics can save the day. Consider the following:

> A miniature gumball machine contains 7 blue, 5 green, and 4 red gumballs, which are identical except for their colors. If the machine dispenses three gumballs at random, what is the probability that it dispenses one gumball of each color?

Consider one specific case: blue first, then green, then red. By the domino-effect rule, the probability of this case is $\dfrac{7\,\text{blue}}{16\,\text{total}} \times \dfrac{5\,\text{green}}{15\,\text{total}} \times \dfrac{4\,\text{red}}{14\,\text{total}} = \dfrac{\cancel{7}}{\cancel{16}\,4} \times \dfrac{\cancel{5}}{\cancel{15}\,3} \times \dfrac{\cancel{4}}{\cancel{14}\,2} = \dfrac{1}{24}$.

Now consider another case: green first, then red, then blue. The probability of this case is $\dfrac{5\,\text{green}}{16\,\text{total}} \times \dfrac{4\,\text{red}}{15\,\text{total}} \times \dfrac{7\,\text{blue}}{14\,\text{total}} = \dfrac{\cancel{5}}{\cancel{16}\,4} \times \dfrac{\cancel{4}}{\cancel{15}\,3} \times \dfrac{\cancel{7}}{\cancel{14}\,2} = \dfrac{1}{24}$. Notice that the probability is the same! This is no accident; the order in which the balls come out does not matter. The three numerators will always be 7, 5, and 4, and the three denominators will always be 16, 15, and 14.

Because the three desired gumballs can come out in any order, there are 3!, or 6, different cases. *All of these cases have the same probability.* Therefore, the overall probability is $6 \times \dfrac{1}{24} = \dfrac{1}{4}$.

In general, when you have a symmetrical problem (a problem with multiple equivalent cases), calculate the probability of one case (often by using the domino-effect rule). Then multiply by the number of cases. Use combinatorics to calculate the number of cases, if necessary.

7

When you apply a symmetry argument, the situation must truly be symmetrical. In the case above, if you swapped the order of "red" and "green" emerging from the gumball machine, nothing would change about the problem. As a result, you can use symmetry to simplify the computation.

Probability Trees

Trees can be a useful tool to keep track of branching possibilities and winning scenarios. Consider the following problem:

> Renee has a bag of 6 candies, 4 of which are sweet and 2 of which are sour. Jack picks two candies simultaneously and at random. What is the chance that exactly one of the candies he has picked is sour?

Even though Jack picks the two candies simultaneously, you can pretend that he picks them in a sequence. This trick allows you to set up a tree reflecting Jack's picks at each stage.

The tree is shown below. Label each branch and put in probabilities. Jack has a $\frac{2}{6}$ chance of picking a sour candy first and a $\frac{4}{6}$ chance of picking a sweet candy first. Note that these probabilities add to 1. On the second set of branches, put the probabilities *as if* Jack has already made his first pick. Remember the domino effect! When making the second pick, don't forget to remove one of the type of candy chosen on the first pick.

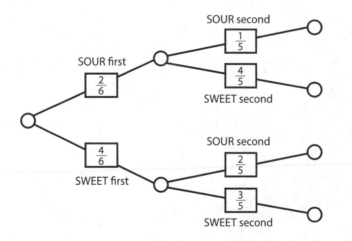

7

Now compute the probabilities of the desired scenarios. One scenario is *sour first* AND *sweet second*; the other is *sweet first* AND *sour second*. Since each scenario is one event AND another event occurring together, multiply the basic probabilities. In other words, you multiply the branches:

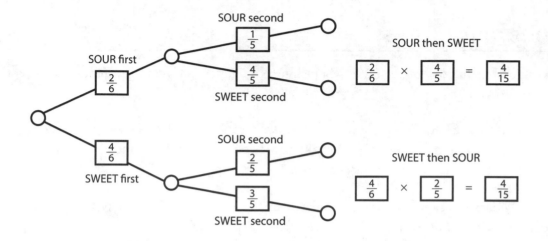

Finally, EITHER one scenario OR the other scenario works: in either case, Jack picks exactly one sour candy. Add these probabilities: $\dfrac{4}{15} + \dfrac{4}{15} = \dfrac{8}{15}$.

Problem Set

1. Three gnomes and three elves sit down in a row of six chairs. If no gnome will sit next to another gnome and no elf will sit next to another elf, in how many different ways can the elves and gnomes sit?

2. Gordon buys 5 dolls for his 5 nieces. The gifts include 2 identical Sun-and-Fun beach dolls, 1 Elegant Eddie dress-up doll, 1 G.I. Josie army doll, and 1 Tulip Troll doll. If the youngest niece does not want the G.I. Josie doll, in how many different ways can he give the gifts?

3. Every morning, Grishma walks from her house to the bus stop; the placement of the house and bus stop are shown in the diagram to the right. She always travels exactly nine blocks from her house to the bus, but she varies the route she takes every day. (One sample route is shown.) How many days can Grishma walk from her house to the bus stop without repeating the same route?

4. In a bag of marbles, there are 3 red, 2 white, and 5 blue marbles. If Kia takes 2 marbles out of the bag, what is the probability that he will have 1 white and 1 blue marble? (Assume that Kia does not replace the marbles in the bag.)

5. A florist has 2 azaleas, 3 buttercups, and 4 petunias. She puts two flowers together at random in a bouquet. However, the customer calls and says that she does not want two of the same flower. What is the probability that the florist does not have to change the bouquet?

6. Five A-list actresses are vying for the three leading roles in the new film "Catfight" in Denmark. The actresses are Julia Robards, Meryl Strep, Sally Fieldstone, Nicole Kadman, and Hallie Strawberry. Assuming that no actress has any advantage in getting any role, what is the probability that Julia and Hallie will star in the film together?

7

7. For one roll of a certain number cube with six faces, numbered 1 through 6, the

    probability of rolling a two is $\frac{1}{6}$. If this number cube is rolled 4 times, which of the

    following is the probability that the outcome will be a two *at least* 3 times?

    (A) $\left(\dfrac{1}{6}\right)^4$

    (B) $2\left(\dfrac{1}{6}\right)^3 + \left(\dfrac{1}{6}\right)^4$

    (C) $3\left(\dfrac{1}{6}\right)^3\left(\dfrac{5}{6}\right) + \left(\dfrac{1}{6}\right)^4$

    (D) $4\left(\dfrac{1}{6}\right)^3\left(\dfrac{5}{6}\right) + \left(\dfrac{1}{6}\right)^4$

    (E) $6\left(\dfrac{1}{6}\right)^3\left(\dfrac{5}{6}\right) + \left(\dfrac{1}{6}\right)^4$

7

Solutions

1. 72: The only way to ensure that no two gnomes and no two elves sit next to each other is to have the gnomes and elves alternate seats (GEGEGE or EGEGEG). Use the slot method to assign seats to gnomes or elves. Begin by seating the first gnome. As he is the first to be seated, he can sit anywhere. He has 6 choices. If the first gnome sits in an odd-numbered chair, the second gnome can sit in either of the two remaining odd-numbered chairs. (Likewise, if the first gnome sits in an even-numbered chair, the second gnome can sit in either

Person	Choices	Seat Assigned
Gnome A	6 choices (1, 2, 3, 4, 5, 6)	#1
Gnome B	2 choices (3, 5)	#3
Gnome C	1 choice (5)	#5
Elf A	3 choices (2, 4, 6)	#2
Elf B	2 choices (4, 6)	#4
Elf C	1 choice (6)	#6

of the two remaining even-numbered chairs.) Either way, the second gnome has two choices. The last gnome has only 1 chair option, since she is not to be seated next to another gnome.

Then, seat the elves. The first elf can sit in any of the three empty chairs, the second in any of the other two, and the last in the final remaining chair. Therefore, the first elf has three choices, the second elf has two choices, and the third elf has one choice.

Finally, find the product of the number of choices for each "person":

$$6 \times 2 \times 1 \times 3 \times 2 \times 1 = 72$$

You can also think of this problem as a succession of three choices: 1) choosing whether to arrange the little guys as GEGEGE or EGEGEG, 2) choosing the order of the gnomes, and then 3) choosing the order of the elves.

The first choice has only two options: EGEGEG and GEGEGE. Each of the subsequent choices has 3!, or 6 options, because those choices involve unrestricted rearrangements (simple factorials). Therefore, the total number of seating arrangements is: $2 \times 3! \times 3! = 2 \times 6 \times 6 = 72$.

2. 48: First, solve the problem without considering the fact that the youngest girl does not want the G.I. Josie doll.

Gordon's nieces could get either one of the Sun-and-Fun dolls, which we'll call S, or they could get the Elegant Eddie doll (E), the Tulip Troll doll (T), or the G.I. Josie doll (G). This problem can be modeled with anagrams for the "word" SSETG:

$$\frac{5!}{2!} = 5 \times 4 \times 3 = 60$$

A	B	C	D	E
S	S	E	T	G

Note that you should divide by 2! because of the two identical Sun-and-Fun dolls.

Thus, there are 60 ways in which Gordon can give the gifts to his nieces.

However, you know that the youngest girl (niece E) does not want the G.I. Josie doll. So, calculate the number of arrangements in which the youngest girl *does* get the G.I. Josie doll. If niece E gets doll G, then you still have 2 S dolls, 1 E doll, and 1 T doll to give out to nieces A, B, C, and D. Model this situation with the anagrams of the "word" SSET:

$$\frac{4!}{2!} = 12$$

A	B	C	D
S	S	E	T

There are 12 ways in which the youngest niece *will* get the G.I. Josie doll.

Therefore, there are 60 − 12, or 48, ways in which Gordon can give the dolls to his nieces.

3. **126 days:** No matter which route Grishma walks, she will travel 4 blocks to the left and 5 blocks down. This can be modeled with the "word" LLLLDDDDD. Find the number of anagrams for this "word":

$$\frac{9!}{5!4!} = \frac{9 \times 8 \times 7 \times 6}{4 \times 3 \times 2 \times 1} = 126$$

This problem can also be solved with the combinations formula. Grishma is going to walk 9 blocks in a row, no matter what. Imagine that those blocks are already marked 1, 2, 3, and 4 (the first block she walks, the second block she walks, and so on), up to 9. Now, to create a route, four of those blocks will be dubbed "Left" and the other five will be "Down." The question is, in how many ways can she assign those labels to the numbered blocks?

The answer is given by the fact that she is choosing a combination of either 4 blocks out of 9 ("Left") or 5 blocks out of 9 ("Down"). (Either method gives the same answer.) At first it may seem as though "order matters" here, because Grishma is choosing routes, but "order" does not matter in the combinatorial sense. That is, designating blocks 1, 2, 3, and 4 as "Left" blocks is the same as designating blocks 3, 2, 4, and 1 as "Left" blocks (or any other order of those same four blocks). Therefore, use combinations, not permutations, to derive the expression: $\frac{9!}{5! \times 4!} = 126$.

4. $\frac{2}{9}$: You can solve this problem by listing the winning scenarios or by using combinatorics counting methods. Both solutions are presented below:

1. List the winning scenarios

First Pick	Second Pick	Probability
(1) Blue $\left(\frac{1}{2}\right)$	White $\left(\frac{2}{9}\right)$	$\frac{1}{2} \times \frac{2}{9} = \frac{1}{9}$
(2) White $\left(\frac{1}{5}\right)$	Blue $\left(\frac{5}{9}\right)$	$\frac{1}{5} \times \frac{5}{9} = \frac{1}{9}$

To find the probability, add the probabilities of the winning scenarios: $\frac{1}{9} + \frac{1}{9} = \frac{2}{9}$.

2. Use the counting method

A	B	C	D	E	F	G	H	I	J
Y	Y	N	N	N	N	N	N	N	N

There are $\dfrac{10!}{2!8!} = 45$ different combinations of marbles.

Since there are 2 white marbles and 5 blue marbles, there are $2 \times 5 = 10$ different white–blue combinations. Therefore, the probability of selecting a blue and white combination is $\dfrac{10}{45}$, or $\dfrac{2}{9}$.

5. $\dfrac{13}{18}$: Solve this problem by finding the probability that the two flowers in the bouquet *will* be the same, and then subtract the result from 1. The table to the right indicates that there are 10 different bouquets in which both flowers are the same. Then, find the number of different 2-flower bouquets that can be made in total, using an anagram model. In how many different ways can you arrange the letters in the "word" YYNNNNNNN?

Flower #1	Flower #2
A_1	A_2
B_1	B_2
B_1	B_3
B_2	B_3
P_1	P_2
P_1	P_3
P_1	P_4
P_2	P_3
P_2	P_4
P_3	P_4

$$\frac{9!}{7!2!} = \frac{9 \times 8}{2 \times 1} = 36$$

The probability of randomly putting together a bouquet that contains two of the same type of flower is $\dfrac{10}{36}$, or $\dfrac{5}{18}$. Therefore, the probability of randomly putting together a bouquet that contains two different flowers and that therefore will *not* need to be changed is $1 - \dfrac{5}{18}$, or $\dfrac{13}{18}$.

6. $\dfrac{3}{10}$: The probability of Julia being cast first is $\dfrac{1}{5}$. If Julia is cast, the probability of Hallie being cast second is $\dfrac{1}{4}$. The probability of any of the remaining 3 actresses being cast is $\dfrac{3}{3}$, or 1. Therefore, the probability of this chain of events is:

$$\frac{1}{5} \times \frac{1}{4} \times 1 = \frac{1}{20}$$

There are six event chains that yield this outcome, shown in the chart to the right. Therefore, the total probability that Julia and Hallie will be among the 3 leading actresses is:

$$\frac{1}{20} \times 6 = \frac{6}{20} = \frac{3}{10}$$

Actress (1)	Actress (2)	Actress (3)
Julia	Hallie	X
Julia	X	Hallie
Hallie	Julia	X
Hallie	X	Julia
X	Julia	Hallie
X	Hallie	Julia

7

Alternatively, you can solve this problem with counting methods.

The number of different combinations in which the actresses can be cast in the roles, assuming you are not concerned with which actress is given which role, is $\frac{5!}{3!2!} = 5 \times 2 = 10$.

A	B	C	D	E
Y	Y	N	N	N

There are 3 possible combinations that feature both Julia and Hallie:

(1) Julia, Hallie, Sally
(2) Julia, Hallie, Meryl
(3) Julia, Hallie, Nicole

Therefore, the probability that Julia and Hallie will star together is $\frac{3}{10}$.

7. **(D):** $4\left(\frac{1}{6}\right)^3\left(\frac{5}{6}\right) + \left(\frac{1}{6}\right)^4$

Unfortunately, you cannot easily use the $1 - x$ trick here, so you must express the probability directly. You must regard the desired outcome in two separate parts: first, rolling a two *exactly* 4 times, and second, rolling a two *exactly* 3 times out of 4 attempts. First, the probability of rolling a two *exactly* 4 times is $\left(\frac{1}{6}\right)\left(\frac{1}{6}\right)\left(\frac{1}{6}\right)\left(\frac{1}{6}\right) = \left(\frac{1}{6}\right)^4$.

Next, if you roll a two exactly 3 times out of 4 attempts, then on exactly one of those attempts, you do *not* roll a two. Hence, the probability of rolling a two exactly 3 times out of 4 attempts is the sum of the following four probabilities:

Outcome		Probability
(Two)(Two)(Two)(Not a Two)	→	$\left(\frac{1}{6}\right)\left(\frac{1}{6}\right)\left(\frac{1}{6}\right)\left(\frac{5}{6}\right) = \left(\frac{1}{6}\right)^3\left(\frac{5}{6}\right)$
(Two)(Two)(Not a Two)(Two)	→	$\left(\frac{1}{6}\right)\left(\frac{1}{6}\right)\left(\frac{5}{6}\right)\left(\frac{1}{6}\right) = \left(\frac{1}{6}\right)^3\left(\frac{5}{6}\right)$
(Two)(Not a Two)(Two)(Two)	→	$\left(\frac{1}{6}\right)\left(\frac{5}{6}\right)\left(\frac{1}{6}\right)\left(\frac{1}{6}\right) = \left(\frac{1}{6}\right)^3\left(\frac{5}{6}\right)$
(Not a Two)(Two)(Two)(Two)	→	$\left(\frac{5}{6}\right)\left(\frac{1}{6}\right)\left(\frac{1}{6}\right)\left(\frac{1}{6}\right) = \left(\frac{1}{6}\right)^3\left(\frac{5}{6}\right)$
		$4\left(\frac{1}{6}\right)^3\left(\frac{5}{6}\right)$

Notice that there are 4 rearrangements of 3 "Twos" and 1 "Not a two." In other words, you have to count as separate outcomes the 4 different positions in which the "Not a two" roll occurs: first, second, third, or fourth.

There is no way to roll a two exactly 4 times AND exactly 3 times, so you can now just add up these probabilities. Thus, the desired probability is $4\left(\frac{1}{6}\right)^3\left(\frac{5}{6}\right) + \left(\frac{1}{6}\right)^4$.

MANHATTAN
PREP

Appendix A *of*
Number Properties

Data Sufficiency

In This Chapter...

Appendix A
Data Sufficiency

Data Sufficiency (DS) problems are a cross between math and logic. Imagine that your boss just walked into your office and dumped a bunch of papers on your desk, saying, "Hey, our client wants to know whether they should raise the price on this product. Can you answer that question from this data? If so, which pieces do we need to prove the case?" What would you do?

The client has asked a specific question: should the company raise the price? You have to decide which pieces of information will allow you to answer that question—or, possibly, that you don't have enough information to answer the question at all.

This kind of logical reasoning is exactly what you use when you answer DS questions.

How Data Sufficiency Works

If you already feel comfortable with the basics of Data Sufficiency, you may want to move quickly through this particular section of the chapter—but you are encouraged to read it. There are a few insights that you may find useful.

Every DS problem has the same basic form:

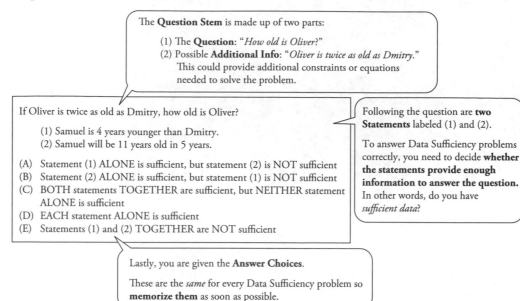

The **Question Stem** is made up of two parts:

(1) The **Question**: "*How old is Oliver?*"
(2) Possible **Additional Info**: "*Oliver is twice as old as Dmitry.*"
   This could provide additional constraints or equations
   needed to solve the problem.

If Oliver is twice as old as Dmitry, how old is Oliver?

(1) Samuel is 4 years younger than Dmitry.
(2) Samuel will be 11 years old in 5 years.

(A) Statement (1) ALONE is sufficient, but statement (2) is NOT sufficient
(B) Statement (2) ALONE is sufficient, but statement (1) is NOT sufficient
(C) BOTH statements TOGETHER are sufficient, but NEITHER statement ALONE is sufficient
(D) EACH statement ALONE is sufficient
(E) Statements (1) and (2) TOGETHER are NOT sufficient

Following the question are **two Statements** labeled (1) and (2).

To answer Data Sufficiency problems correctly, you need to decide **whether the statements provide enough information to answer the question.** In other words, do you have *sufficient data*?

Lastly, you are given the **Answer Choices.**

These are the *same* for every Data Sufficiency problem so **memorize them** as soon as possible.

The question stem contains the question you need to answer. The two statements provide *given* information, information that is true. DS questions look strange but you can think of them as deconstructed Problem Solving (PS) questions. Compare the DS-format problem above to the PS-format problem below:

Samuel is 4 years younger than Dmitry, and Samuel will be 11 years old in 5 years.
If Oliver is twice as old as Dmitry, how old is Oliver?"

The two questions contain exactly the same information; that information is just presented in a different order. The PS question stem contains all of the givens as well as the question. The DS problem moves some of the givens down to statement (1) and statement (2).

As with regular PS problems, the given information in the DS statements is always true. In addition, the two statements won't contradict each other. In the same way that a PS question wouldn't tell you that $x > 0$ *and* $x < 0$, the two DS statements won't do that either.

In the PS format, you would go ahead and calculate Oliver's age. The DS format works a bit differently. Here is the full problem, including the answer choices:

If Oliver is twice as old as Dmitry, how old is Oliver?

(1) Samuel is 4 years younger than Dmitry.
(2) Samuel will be 11 years old in 5 years.

(A) Statement (1) ALONE is sufficient, but statement (2) is NOT sufficient.
(B) Statement (2) ALONE is sufficient, but statement (1) is NOT sufficient.
(C) BOTH statements TOGETHER are sufficient, but NEITHER statement ALONE is sufficient.
(D) EACH statement ALONE is sufficient.
(E) Statements (1) and (2) TOGETHER are NOT sufficient.

Despite all appearances, the question is not actually asking you to calculate Oliver's age. Rather, it's asking *which pieces of information* would allow you to calculate Oliver's age.

You may already be able solve this one on your own, but you'll see much harder problems on the test, so your first task is to learn how to work through DS questions in a systematic, consistent way.

As you think the problem through, jot down information from the question stem:

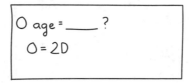

Hmm. If they tell you Dmitry's age, then you can find Oliver's age. Remember that!

Take a look at the first statement. Also, write down the $\frac{AD}{BCE}$ answer grid (you'll learn why as you work through the problem):

(1) Samuel is 4 years younger than Dmitry.

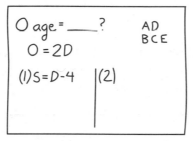

The first statement doesn't allow you to figure out anyone's real age. Statement (1), then, is *not suffi-cient.* Now you can cross off the top row of answers, (A) and (D).

Why? Here's the text for answers (A) and (D):

   (A) Statement (1) ALONE is sufficient, but statement (2) is NOT sufficient.
   (D) EACH statement ALONE is sufficient.

Both answers indicate that statement (1) is sufficient to answer the question. Because statement (1) is *not* sufficient to find Oliver's age, both (A) and (D) are wrong.

The answer choices will always appear in the order shown for the above problem, so any time you decide that statement (1) is not sufficient, you will always cross off answers (A) and (D). That's why your answer grid groups these two answers together.

Next, consider statement (2), but remember one tricky thing: forget what statement (1) told you. Because of the way DS is constructed, you must evaluate the two statements separately before you look at them together:

(2) Samuel will be 11 years old in 5 years.

It's useful to write the two statements side-by-side, as shown above, to help remember that statement (2) is separate from statement (1) and has to be considered by itself first.

Statement (2) does indicate how old Sam is now, but says nothing about Oliver or Dmitry. (Remember, you're looking *only* at statement (2) now.) By itself, statement (2) is not sufficient, so cross off answer (B).

Now that you've evaluated each statement by itself, take a look at the two statements together. Statement (2) provides Sam's age, and statement (1) allows you to calculate Dmitry's age if you know Sam's age. Finally, the question stem allows you to calculate Oliver's age if you know Dmitry's age:

As soon as you can tell that you *can* solve, put down a check mark or write an S with a circle around it (or both!). Don't actually calculate Oliver's age; the GMAT doesn't give you any extra time to calculate a number that you don't need.

The correct answer is **(C)**.

MANHATTAN
PREP

The Answer Choices

The five Data Sufficiency answer choices will always be exactly the same (and presented in the same order), so memorize them before you go into the test.

Here are the five answers written in an easier way to understand:

> (A) Statement (1) does allow you to answer the question, but statement (2) does not.
> (B) Statement (2) does allow you to answer the question, but statement (1) does not.
> (C) Neither statement works on its own, but you can use them *together* to answer the question.
> (D) Statement (1) works by itself *and* statement (2) works by itself.
> (E) Nothing works. Even if you use both statements together, you still can't answer the question.

Answer (C) specifically says that neither statement works on its own. For this reason, you are required to look at each statement by itself *and decide that neither one works* before you are allowed to evaluate the two statements together.

Here's an easier way to remember the five answer choices; we call this the "twelve-ten" mnemonic (memory aid):

1	only statement 1
2	only statement 2
T	together
E	either one
N	neither/nothing

Within the next week, memorize the DS answers. If you do a certain number of practice DS problems in that time frame, you'll likely memorize the answers without conscious effort—and you'll solidify the DS lessons you're learning right now.

Starting with Statement (2)

If statement (1) looks hard, start with statement (2) instead. Your process will be the same, except you'll make one change in your answer grid.

Try this problem:

> If Oliver is twice as old as Dmitry, how old is Oliver?
>
> (1) Two years ago, Dmitry was twice as old as Samuel.
> (2) Samuel is 6 years old.

(From now on, the answer choices won't be shown. Start memorizing!)

Statement (1) is definitely more complicated than statement (2), so start with statement (2) instead. Change your answer grid to $\frac{BD}{ACE}$. (You'll learn why in a minute.)

(2) Samuel is 6 years old.

Statement (2) is not sufficient to determine Oliver's age, so cross off the answers that say statement (2) is sufficient: (B) and (D). Once again, you can cross off the entire top row; when starting with statement (2), you always will keep or eliminate these two choices at the same time.

Now assess statement (1):

(1) Two years ago, Dmitry was twice as old as Samuel.

Forget all about statement (2); only statement (1) exists. By itself, is the statement sufficient?

Nope! Too many variables. Cross off (A), the first of the remaining answers in the bottom row, and assess the two statements together:

You can plug Samuel's age (from the second statement) into the formula from statement (1) to find Dmitry's age, and then use Dmitry's age to find Oliver's age. Together, the statements are sufficient.

The correct answer is **(C)**.

The two answer grids work in the same way, regardless of which one you use. As long as you use the AD/BCE grid when starting with statement (1), or the BD/ACE grid when starting with statement (2), you will always:

- cross off the *top* row if the first statement you try is *not* sufficient;
- cross off the *bottom* row if the first statement you try *is* sufficient; and
- assess the remaining row of answers one answer at a time.

Finally, remember that you must assess the statements separately before you can try them together—and you'll only try them together if neither one is sufficient on its own. You will only consider the two together if you have already crossed off answers (A), (B), and (D).

Value vs. Yes/No Questions

Data Sufficiency questions come in two "flavors": Value or Yes/No.

On Value questions, it is necessary to find a single value in order to answer the question. If you can't find any value or you can find two or more values, then the information is not sufficient.

Consider this statement:

> (1) Oliver's age is a multiple of 4.

Oliver could be 4 or 8 or 12 or any age that is a multiple of 4. Because it's impossible to determine one particular value for Oliver's age, the statement is not sufficient

What if the question changed?

> Is Oliver's age an even number?
>
> (1) Oliver's age is a multiple of 4.
> (2) Oliver is between 19 and 23 years old.

This question is a Yes/No question. There are three possible answers to a Yes/No question:

1. Always Yes: Sufficient!
2. Always No: Sufficient!
3. Maybe (or Sometimes Yes, Sometimes No): Not Sufficient

It may surprise you that Always No is sufficient to answer the question. Imagine that you ask a friend to go to the movies with you. If she says, "No, I'm sorry, I can't," then you did receive an answer to your question (even though the answer is negative). You know she can't go to the movies with you.

Apply this reasoning to the Oliver question. Is statement 1 sufficient to answer the question *Is Oliver's age an even number?*

> (1) Oliver's age is a multiple of 4.

If Oliver's age is a multiple of 4, then Yes, he must be an even number of years old. The information isn't enough to tell how old Oliver actually is—he could be 4, 8, 12, or any multiple of 4 years old. Still, the information is sufficient to answer the specific question asked.

Because the statement tried first is sufficient, cross off the bottom row of answers, (B), (C), and (E).

Next, check statement (2):

> (2) Oliver is between 19 and 23 years old.

Oliver could be 20, in which case his age is even. He could also be 21, in which case his age is odd. The answer here is Sometimes Yes, Sometimes No, so the information is not sufficient to answer the question.

The correct answer is **(A)**: the first statement is sufficient but the second is not.

The DS Process

This section summarizes everything you've learned in one consistent DS process. You can use this on every DS problem on the test.

Step 1: Determine whether the question is Value or Yes/No.

Value: The question asks for the value of an unknown (e.g., What is x?).

A statement is **Sufficient** when it provides **1 possible value**.

A statement is **Not Sufficient** when it provides **more than 1 possible value** (or none at all).

Yes/No: The question asks whether a given piece of information is true (e.g., Is x even?). Most of the time, these will be in the form of Yes/No questions.

A statement is **Sufficient** when the answer is **Always Yes** or **Always No**.

A statement is **Not Sufficient** when the answer is **Maybe** or **Sometimes Yes, Sometimes No**.

Step 2: Separate given information from the question itself.

If the question stem contains given information—that is, any information other than the question itself—then write down that information separately from the question itself. This is true information that you must consider or use when answering the question.

Step 3: Rephrase the question.

Most of the time, you will not write down the entire question stem exactly as it appears on screen. At the least, you'll simplify what is written on screen. For example, if the question stem asks, "What is the value of x?" then you might write down something like $x =$ _____?

For more complicated question stems, you may have more work to do. Ideally, before you go to the statements, you will be able to articulate a fairly clear and straightforward question. In the earlier example, $x =$ _____? is clear and straightforward.

What if this is the question?

If $xyz \neq 0$, is $\dfrac{3x}{2} + y + 2z = \dfrac{7x}{2} + y$?

(1) $y = 3$ and $x = 2$
(2) $z = -x$

Do you need to know the individual values of x, y, and z in order to answer the question? Would knowing the value of a combination of the variables, such as $x + y + z$, work? It's tough to tell.

In order to figure this out, **rephrase** the question stem, which is a fancy way of saying: simplify the information a lot. Take the time to do this before you address the statements; you'll make your job much easier!

If you're given an equation, the first task is to put the "like" variables together. Also, when working with the question stem, make sure to carry the question mark through your work:

$$y - y + 2z = \dfrac{7x}{2} - \dfrac{3x}{2}?$$

That's interesting: the two y variables cancel out. Keep simplifying:

$$2z = \dfrac{4x}{2}?$$
$$2z = 2x?$$
$$z = x?$$

That whole crazy equation is really asking a much simpler question: is $z = x$?

It might seem silly to keep writing that question mark at the end of each line, but don't skip that step or you'll be opening yourself up to a careless error. By the time you get to the end, you don't want to forget that this is still a *question*, not a statement or given.

Step 4: Use the Answer Grid to Evaluate the Statements

If you start with statement 1, then write the AD/BCE grid on your scrap paper.

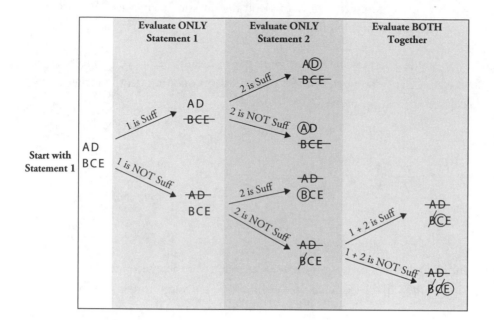

Here is the rephrased problem:

If $xyz \neq 0$, is $z = x$?

(1) $y = 3$ and $x = 2$

(2) $z = -x$

Statement (1) is useless by itself because it says nothing about z. Cross off the top row of answers: $\dfrac{\text{A̶D̶}}{\text{BCE}}$

Statement (2) turns out to be very useful. None of the variables is 0, so if $z = -x$, then those two numbers cannot be equal to each other. This statement is sufficient to answer the question: no, z does not equal x. You can circle B on your grid: $\dfrac{\text{A̶D̶}}{\text{B̶CE}}$

The correct answer is **(B)**.

If you decide to start with statement (2), your process is almost identical, but you'll use the BD/ACE grid instead. For example:

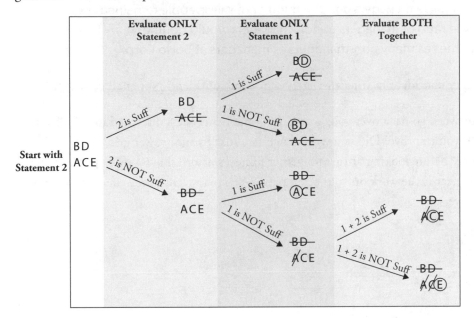

First, evaluate statement (1) by itself and, if you've crossed off answers (A), (B), and (D), then evaluate the two statements together.

Whether you use AD/BCE or BD/ACE, remember to

- cross off the *top* row if the first statement you try is *not* sufficient, and
- cross off the *bottom* row if the first statement you try *is* sufficient.

Pop Quiz! Test Your Skills

Have you learned the DS process? If not, go back through the chapter and work through the sample problems again. Try writing out each step yourself.

If so, prove it! Give yourself up to four minutes total to try the following two problems:

1. Are there more engineers than salespeople working at SoHo Corp?

    (1) SoHo Corp employs $\frac{2}{3}$ as many clerical staff as engineers and salespeople combined.
    (2) If 3 more engineers were employed by SoHo Corp and the number of salespeople remained the same, then the number of engineers would be double the number of salespeople employed by the company.

2. At SoHo Corp, what is the ratio of managers to non-managers?

   (1) If there were 3 more managers and the number of salespeople remained the same, then the ratio of managers to non-managers would double.
   (2) There are 4 times as many non-managers as managers at SoHo Corp.

How did it go? Are you very confident in your answers? Somewhat confident? Not at all confident?

Before you check your answers, go back over your work, using the DS process discussed in this chapter as your guide. Where can you improve? Did you write down (and use!) your answer grid? Did you look at each statement separately before looking at them together (if necessary)? Did you mix up any of the steps of the process? How neat is the work on your scrap paper? You may want to rewrite your work before you review the answers.

Pop Quiz Answer Key

1. Engineers vs. Salespeople

Step 1: Is this a Value or Yes/No question?

   1. Are there more engineers than salespeople working at SoHo Corp?

This is a Yes/No question.

Steps 2 and 3: What is given and what is the question? Rephrase the question.

The question stem doesn't contain any given information. In this case, the question is already about as simplified as it can get: are there more engineers than salespeople?

Step 4: Evaluate the statements.

If you start with the first statement, use the AD/BCE answer grid.

   (1) SoHo Corp employs $\frac{2}{3}$ as many clerical staff as engineers and salespeople combined.

If you add up the engineers and salespeople, then there are fewer people on the clerical staff...but this indicates nothing about the relative number of engineers and salespeople. This statement is not sufficient. Cross off (A) and (D), the top row, of your answer grid.

   (2) If 3 more engineers were employed by SoHo Corp and the number of salespeople remained the same, then the number of engineers would be double the number of salespeople employed by the company.

This one sounds promising. If you add only 3 engineers, then you'll have twice as many engineers as salespeople. Surely, that means there are more engineers than salespeople?

Don't jump to any conclusions. Test some possible numbers; think about fairly extreme scenarios. What if you start with just 1 engineer? When you add 3, you'll have 4 engineers. If there are 4 engineers, then there are half as many, or 2, salespeople. In other words, you start with 1 engineer and 2 salespeople, so there are more salespeople. Interesting.

According to this one case, the answer to the Yes/No question *Are there more engineers than salespeople?* is no.

Can you find a yes answer? Try a larger set of numbers. If you start with 11 engineers and add 3, then you would have 14 total. The number of salespeople would have to be 7. In this case, then, there are more engineers to start than salespeople, so the answer to the question *Are there more engineers than salespeople?* is yes.

Because you can find both yes and no answers, statement (2) is not sufficient. Cross off answer (B).

Now, try the two statements together. How does the information about the clerical staff combine with statement (2)?

Whenever you're trying some numbers and you have to examine the two statements together, see whether you can reuse the numbers that you tried earlier.

If you start with 1 engineer, you'll have 2 salespeople, for a total of 3. In this case, you'd have 2 clerical staff, and the answer to the original question is no.

If you start with 11 engineers, you'll have 7 salespeople, for a total of 18. In this case, you'd have 12 clerical staff, and the answer to the original question is yes.

The correct answer is **(E)**. The information is not sufficient even when both statements are used together.

2. Managers vs. Non-Managers

Step 1: Is this a Value or a Yes/No question?

> 2. At SoHo Corp, what is the ratio of managers to non-managers?

This is a Value question. You need to find one specific ratio—or know that you can find one specific ratio—in order to answer the question.

Steps 2 and 3: What is given and what is the question? Rephrase the question.

Find the ratio of managers to non-managers, or M : N.

Step 4: Evaluate the statements.

If you start with the second statement, use the BD/ACE answer grid. (Note: this is always your choice; the solution with the BD/ACE grid shown is just for practice.)

> (2) There are 4 times as many non-managers as managers at SoHo Corp.

If there is 1 manager, there are 4 non-managers. If there are 2 managers, there are 8 non-managers. If there are 3 managers, there are 12 non-managers.

What does that mean? In each case, the ratio of managers to non-managers is the same, $1:4$. Even though you don't know how many managers and non-managers there are, you do know the ratio. (For more on ratios, see the Ratios chapter of the *Fractions, Decimals, & Percents GMAT Strategy Guide.*)

This statement is sufficient; cross (A), (C), and (E), the bottom row, off of the grid.

> (1) If there were 3 more managers and the number of salespeople remained the same, then the ratio of managers to non-managers would double.

First, what does it mean to *double* a ratio? If the starting ratio were $2:3$, then doubling that ratio would give you $4:3$. The first number in the ratio doubles relative to the second number.

Test some cases. If you start with 1 manager, then 3 more would bring the total number of managers to 4. The *manager* part of the ratio just quadrupled (1 to 4), not doubled, so this number is not a valid starting point. Discard this case.

If you have to add 3 and want that number to double, then you need to start with 3 managers. When you add 3 more, that portion of the ratio doubles from 3 to 6. The other portion, the non-managers, remains the same.

Notice anything? The statement says nothing about the relative number of non-managers. The starting ratio could be $3:2$ or $3:4$ or $3:14$, for all you know. In each case, doubling the number of managers would double the ratio (to $6:2$, or $6:4$, or $6:14$). You can't figure out the specific ratio from this statement.

The correct answer is **(B)**: statement (2) is sufficient, but statement (1) is not.

Proving Insufficiency

The Pop Quiz solutions used the Testing Cases strategy: testing real numbers to help determine whether a statement is sufficient. You can do this whenever the problem allows for the possibility of multiple numbers or cases.

When you're doing this, your goal is to try to prove the statement insufficient. For example:

> If *x* and *y* are positive integers, is the sum of *x* and *y* between 20 and 26, inclusive?
>
> (1) $x - y = 6$

Test your first case. You're allowed to pick any numbers for *x* and *y* that make statement 1 true *and* that follow any constraints given in the question stem. In this case, that means the two numbers have to be positive integers and that $x - y$ has to equal 6.

Case #1: $20 - 14 = 6$. These numbers make statement 1 true and follow the constraint in the question stem, so these are legal numbers to pick. Now, try to answer the Yes/No question: $20 + 14 = 34$, so no, the sum is not between 20 and 26, inclusive.

You now have a *no* answer. Can you think of another set of numbers that will give you the opposite, a *yes* answer?

Case #2: $15 - 9 = 6$. In this case, the sum is 24, so the answer to the Yes/No question is yes, the sum is between 20 and 26, inclusive.

Because you have found both a yes and a no answer, the statement is not sufficient.

Here's a summary of the process:

1. Notice that you can test cases. You can do this when the problem allows for multiple possible values.

2. Pick numbers that make the statement true and that follow any givens in the question stem. If you realize that you picked numbers that make the statement false or contradict givens in the question stem, *discard* those numbers and start over.

3. Your first case will give you one answer: a yes or a no on a Yes/No problem, or a numerical value on a value problem.

4. Try to find a second case that gives you a *different* answer. On a Yes/No problem, you'll be looking for the opposite of what you found for the first case. For a Value problem, you'll be looking for a different numerical answer. (Don't forget that whatever you pick still has to make the statement true and follow the givens in the question stem!)

The usefulness of trying to prove insufficiency is revealed as soon as you find two different answers. You're done! That statement is not sufficient, so you can cross off an answer or answers and move to the next step.

What if you keep finding the same answer? Try this:

> If x and y are positive integers, is the product of x and y between 20 and 26, inclusive?
>
> (1) x is a multiple of 17.

Case #1: Test $x = 17$. Since y must be a positive integer, try the smallest possible value first: $y = 1$. In this case, the product is 17, which is not between 20 and 26 inclusive. The answer to the question is *no*; can you find the opposite answer?

Case #2: If you make $x = 34$, then xy will be too big, so keep $x = 17$. The next smallest possible value for y is 2. In this case, the product is 34, which is also not between 20 and 26 inclusive. The answer is again no.

Can you think of a case where you will get a *yes* answer? No! The smallest possible product is 17, and the next smallest possible product is 34. Any additional values of x and y you try will be equal to or larger than 34.

You've just proved the statement sufficient because it is impossible to find a yes answer. Testing Cases can help you to figure out the "theory" answer, or the mathematical reasoning that proves the statement is sufficient.

This won't always work so cleanly. Sometimes, you'll keep getting all no answers or all yes answers but you won't be able to figure out the theory behind it all. If you test three or four different cases, and you're actively seeking out the opposite answer but never find it, then go ahead and assume that the statement is sufficient, even if you're not completely sure why.

Do make sure that you're trying numbers with different characteristics. Try both even and odd. Try a prime number. Try zero or a negative or a fraction. (You can only try numbers that are allowed by the problem, of course. In the case of the above problems, you were only allowed to try positive integers.)

Here's how Testing Cases would work on a Value problem:

> If x and y are prime numbers, what is the product of x and y?
>
> (1) The product is even.

Case #1: $x = 2$ and $y = 3$. Both numbers are prime numbers and their product is even, so these are legal numbers to try. In this case, the product is 6. Can you choose numbers that will give a different product?

Case #2: $x = 2$ and $y = 5$. Both numbers are prime numbers and their product is even, so these are legal numbers to try. In this case, the product is 10.

The statement is not sufficient because there are at least two different values for the product of x and y.

In short, when you're evaluating DS statements, go into them with an "I'm going to try to prove you insufficient!" mindset.

- If you do find two different answers (yes and no, or two different numbers), then immediately declare that statement not sufficient.

- If, after several tries, you keep finding the same answer despite trying different kinds of numbers, see whether you can articulate why; that statement may be sufficient after all. Even if you can't say why, go ahead and assume that the statement is sufficient.

Now you're ready to test your Data Sufficiency skills. As you work through the chapters in this book, test your progress using some of the *Official Guide* problem set lists found online, in your Manhattan Prep Student Center. Start with lower-numbered problems first, in order to practice the process, and work your way up to more and more difficult problems.

GO BEYOND BOOKS.
TRY A FREE CLASS NOW.

IN-PERSON COURSE

ONLINE COURSE

GMAT® INTERACT™

Find a GMAT course near you and attend the first session free, no strings attached. You'll meet your instructor, learn how the GMAT is scored, review strategies for Data Sufficiency, dive into Sentence Correction, and gain insights into a wide array of GMAT principles and strategies.

Enjoy the flexibility of prepping from home or the office with our online course. Your instructor will cover all the same content and strategies as an in-person course, while giving you the freedom to prep where you want. Attend the first session free to check out our cutting-edge online classroom.

GMAT Interact is a comprehensive self-study program that is fun, intuitive, and driven by you. Each interactive video lesson is taught by an expert instructor and can be accessed on your computer or mobile device. Lessons are personalized for you based on the choices you make.

**Find your city at
manhattanprep.com/gmat/classes**

**See the full schedule at
manhattanprep.com/gmat/classes**

**Try 5 full lessons for free at
manhattanprep.com/gmat/interact**

Not sure which is right for you? Try all three!
Or give us a call and we'll help you figure out
which program fits you best.

Toll-Free U.S. Number (800) 576-4628 | **International** 001 (212) 721-7400 | **Email** gmat@manhattanprep.com

mbaMission

PREP MADE PERSONAL

Whether you want quick coaching in a particular GMAT subject area or a comprehensive study plan developed around your goals, we've got you covered. Our expert, 99th percentile GMAT tutors can help you hit your top score.

CHECK OUT THESE REVIEWS FROM MANHATTAN PREP TUTORING STUDENTS.